T0015949

THE **MINI** ROUGH GUIDE TO
FRANCE

ROUGH GUIDES

YOUR TAILOR-MADE TRIP
STARTS HERE

Tailor-made trips and unique adventures crafted by local experts

Rough Guides has been inspiring travellers for more than 35 years. Leave it to our local experts to create your perfect itinerary and book it at local rates.

Don't follow the crowd – find your own path.

HOW ROUGHGUIDES.COM/TRIPS WORKS

STEP 1 Pick your dream destination, tell us what you want and submit an enquiry.

STEP 2 Fill in a short form to tell your local expert about your dream trip and preferences.

STEP 3 Our local expert will craft your tailor-made itinerary. You'll be able to tweak and refine it until you're completely satisfied.

STEP 4 Book online with ease, pack your bags and enjoy the trip! Our local expert will be on hand 24/7 while you're on the road.

PLAN AND BOOK YOUR TRIP AT
ROUGHGUIDES.COM/TRIPS

HOW TO DOWNLOAD YOUR FREE EBOOK

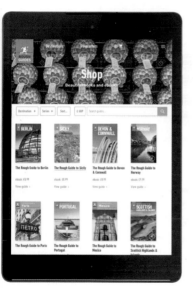

1. Visit **www.roughguides.com/free-ebook** or scan the **QR code** below

2. Enter the code **france559**

3. Follow the simple step-by-step instructions

For troubleshooting contact: mail@roughguides.com

10 THINGS NOT TO MISS

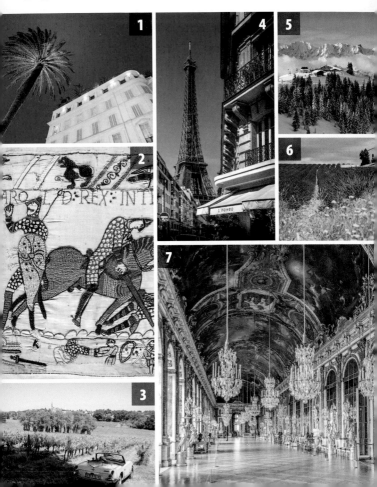

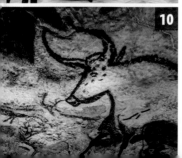

A PERFECT TOUR OF

Day 1

Discover Normandy. Whether approaching from Paris or the Channel ports, our tour starts in Rouen, the home of Impressionism. Begin by exploring its spectacular cathedral and its many historic sights before heading north to the coast to the picturesque port of Honfleur or elegant Deauville. Enjoy the catch-of-the-day at a nearby seafood restaurant.

Day 2

World War II. Head west along the D513 to Caen to visit the memorial museum, which places the D-Day beaches in context. Alternatively continue over the Pegasus Bridge directly to the D-Day beaches. After the poignant experience make your way south to Bayeux to spend two nights.

Day 3

Bayeux Tapestry. Given that the queues can be long make an early start to view the wonderful Bayeux Tapestry. There is, however, more to the town than this treasure, so wander the streets of this ancient place that retains its buildings untouched by war and discover some excellent restaurants. If there is time, go back to the coast on the D6 to the attractive fishing village of Port-en-Bessin.

Day 4

Mont St-Michel. Head out early southwest on the D57 bypassing St-Lô and on to the D999 south to Villedieu-les-Poêles, then take the more scenic D924 to Granville and hug the coast road to Mont-St-Michel. Here you can explore the Benedictine abbey with its spectacular views of the bay. Do not cross by any other route than the causeway as

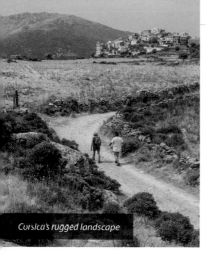

Corsica's rugged landscape

Normandy contribute to the region's popularity as a place to visit. Many painters, understandably, have been drawn to the gentle green countryside, dotted with fields of black-and-white cows under a dramatic and often stormy sky, as well as to the picturesque, colourful fishing ports along the coast.

Further to the west, the craggy coastline and harsh landscape of Brittany continue to evoke the druidical presence of the region's original Celtic roots. Particularly intriguing are the mysterious fields of megaliths and the pink granite rocks of the Corniche Bretonne. Fishing is a major industry in this area.

The subdued Loire Valley, dug out by France's longest river (980km/ 609 miles), remains one of the country's chief tourist attractions. The splendid châteaux and gardens of Touraine are still redolent of the glory of the Ancien Régime and its aristocratic pleasures.

BORDER COUNTRY

To the northeast are the old provinces of Alsace and Lorraine. The Rhineland is the least well defined of the six borders of the hexagon, and the result has been an unending series of nasty territorial disputes between France and Germany over the past few centuries. Alsace was especially valuable because its mines turned France into an important producer of iron ore. The city of Strasbourg, which houses the European Parliament and the Council of Europe, has a German feel in its architecture and its culinary specialities but it remains nonetheless defiantly French. Indeed, that paragon of French patriotism, Joan of Arc, hailed from neighbouring Lorraine, although she was martyred by the English in Rouen.

GEOGRAPHY

France is blessed with an astonishing variety of landscapes: long, high dunes on the Atlantic Coast; craggy coves in Brittany; vineyards in Burgundy; steep gorges in the Tarn Valley; volcanic landscapes in the Auvergne, olive trees, umbrella pines and cypresses in Provence and beautiful beaches in the Côte d'Azur. At around 550,980 sq km (212,735 sq miles), France is the 48th largest country in the world. It

Pretty Honfleur

escaped the gouging glaciers of the Ice Age, so on the whole its landscape is mellow and pastoral, characterised by gentle hills and plateaus, carved by deep river valleys. Imposing mountains lie only along the eastern and southern frontiers. Outside the major urban industrial areas, the rural population is spread thinly over huge areas.

Later geophysical development in the southeastern Garonne region left profound impressions between younger and older hills, providing perfect conditions for the formation of valuable minerals as well as oil and natural gas. To add to France's fortune, an extensive network of rivers, such as the Garonne, provides much fertile agricultural land. Some 34 percent of the land is farmed, and although the economic importance of the agricultural sector is declining, there has been a substantial increase in the number of small organic farms in recent years.

THE NORTHWEST

To the northwest of the country are Brittany and Normandy, each with independent peoples and traditions dating back millennia. The thatched cottages, bent apple trees and locally produced cheeses and ciders of

OVERVIEW

For many years France was a nation of internal contrasts – between the more urban and industrial north and the rural south, between the intellectual élite and the largely agricultural workforce, between chic Paris and the less sophisticated provincial cities – and a nation that saw itself as standing alone, distinct from all others. Much has changed in recent times. Paris is no longer the exclusive Mecca for ambitious young French from the provinces; cities around the country are attracting young professionals who want to escape the more frenetic life in the Ile de France; the number of agricultural workers has shrunk dramatically; industrial and high tech centres have sprung up around the country; provincial cities are developing their own international reputations; and immigration and increasing migration of populations within a 'border-free' European Union are blurring the edges of the French identity.

Quality of life remains a paramount preoccupation. It is no accident that the French are best known for their food and wine, their clothes and perfumes, their art and monumental architecture. Their love of perfection serves them well.

LIE OF THE LAND

France is by far the largest country in Western Europe, a hexagon measuring some 1,000km (620 miles) from north to south and east to west. It is bounded by three seas (the English Channel, the Atlantic and the Mediterranean) and three mountain ranges (the Pyrénées, the Alps and the Jura). The country's four main rivers are: the Loire, running west to the Atlantic from the plateau of the Massif Central; the Seine, flowing northwest from Burgundy through Paris to the Channel; the Garonne, which comes down from the Pyrénées past Toulouse and Bordeaux to the Atlantic; and the Rhône, which starts in the Swiss Alps, then turns south at Lyon and flows down to the Mediterranean.

FOOD AND DRINK `218`

TRAVEL ESSENTIALS `230`

INDEX `252`

HIGHLIGHTS

CONTENTS

NORMANDY & BRITTANY

the tides are rapid and the quicksands dangerous. Continue along the coast road and stay the night in the walled city of St-Malo.

Day 5

Explore Brittany. Spend the day in St Malo, stroll its attractive streets or take a bracing walk with views of the Emerald Coast. Or relax at the elegant resort of Dinard. Then check out the pretty town of Dinan just inland. If it happens to be a Thursday there is a colourful local market.

Days 6-7

Back to nature. Take the faster route via the E50 165km (103 miles) to Morlaix and then the D769 south to Huelgoat and spend a couple of days walking or cycling in the enchanting Parc Régional d'Armorique, staying in a B & B in the pretty little town.

Day 8

Ancient Carnac. Continue (approx. 130km/81 miles) south cross-country on the D769 and finally follow the coast road to Carnac with its fascinating megaliths. Learn more about the ancient stones at the Musée de la Préhistoire. There are plenty of places to spend the night and you can round off the day with a seafood meal.

Day 9

Beachside. Head south to relax on the beach at sophisticated La Baule or, to wind down, visit the fishing port of Le Croisic on the peninsula. If you need to stretch your legs there are some great hiking trails along the rugged coastline.

Located not far south from Strasbourg are the gentle Jura mountains and below them the French Alps, which stretch all the way down to the Alpes Maritimes and Côte d'Azur in the far south of the country. The imposing icy white peak of Mont Blanc, at an impressive 4,810m (15,780ft), is the highest mountain in Europe, and its broad-shouldered shape, once seen, is never forgotten.

WINE COUNTRY

A large number of French towns and provinces are most famous for the high-quality wines that bear their name. Bubbly, for example, is the Champagne region's best-known offering, but the entire northeast is also a major industrial and agricultural region. Similarly, the long river valley running parallel to the eastern frontier and connecting the Saône with the Rhône River not only cradles the vineyards of the regions of Burgundy, Beaujolais and the Rhône, it also aids communication between the north of the country and the south.

SOUTHERN HEARTLAND, CÔTE D'AZUR AND CORSICA

Directly south of the Loire Valley is the enormous Massif Central, which lies in the heart of the country and supplies France with much of its grain. The strange puys of Auvergne (steep conical hills, caused by volcanic eruption during the earth's formation) contrast pleasantly with the rolling hills, plateaux and deep river valleys of neighbouring Périgord and Limousin, located just over to its west.

That the lush Dordogne river valley, in Périgord, has been the site of human settlements for thousands upon thousands of years is evidenced by the

Parlons français !

When Charles de Gaulle died, Noël Coward was asked what he thought God and the General would talk about in heaven. Coward replied: 'That depends on how good God's French is.' Although outdated, the witticism captures French nationalism at its most confident.

prehistoric cave paintings found in its grottoes, particularly the enigmatic depictions of horses, elk and bison surrounded by arrows and strange symbols in the Lascaux cave complex, discovered in 1940 by two boys out walking their dog. Lascaux 4 opened in 2016, a spectacular replica of the paintings housed in a modern centre nearby the original site.

Further south still, basking under blue skies, is the sunny Midi. The landscape here, with its reds, yellows and browns, is very different again, with sun-baked clay buildings and a slower pace of life. That said, not even the south is visually uniform: the wide, yellow fields that seem to stretch forever, the even rows of plane trees and delightful red towns of Languedoc meld into the impossibly verdant Pyrenean mountain range towards the Spanish border, or the Cévennes and Ardèche national parks away to the east.

Many of the old southern cities, such as Toulouse, Montpellier and Nîmes have been quick to embrace the modern age, although there is still an indefinable languor about all of them. Montpellier is perhaps

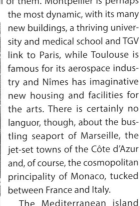

the most dynamic, with its many new buildings, a thriving university and medical school and TGV link to Paris, while Toulouse is famous for its aerospace industry and Nîmes has imaginative new housing and facilities for the arts. There is certainly no languor, though, about the bustling seaport of Marseille, the jet-set towns of the Côte d'Azur and, of course, the cosmopolitan principality of Monaco, tucked between France and Italy.

The Mediterranean island of Corsica not only seems like a separate country to the

Paris

northerner, it would even become one if the independence movement had its way. Its wild, barren landscape, steep cliffs and mountains and lovely beaches make it an interesting destination.

THE CAPITAL

At the country's heart, slightly north of the geographical centre, Paris nestles in a basin that is ideal for industrial and commercial enterprise, comfortably surrounded by the forest and farmland of the Ile-de-France. The city has been called everything from a 'whore' by Henry Miller to 'one of the most noble ornaments of the world' by Montaigne. It remains the centre of everything French and the nexus of French transport (all distances in the country are measured from the square in front of Notre-Dame Cathedral). It is one of the world's great fashion capitals, is revolutionary in its grand arts and architectural projects and also has one of the best-preserved city centres in Europe. It has a distinctive population – stylish, intellectual and reputedly strong minded – and very different from the rural French.

A CULTURAL RESPONSIBILITY

If the land itself is the most obvious source of French pride, the nation's cultural wealth is just as important, as is exporting that wealth to the rest of the world. Philosophy and the fine arts do not strike the French as something to be confined to a small élite. For most people, 'intellectual' is not the dirty word that it seems to be in so many countries. Even the popular arts such as advertising, cinema, comic strips and fashion are elevated to the level of high culture.

An active government cultural policy has preserved the architectural monuments of the *Patrimoine National* from the ravages of time, weather, war, revolution and urban development. France's leaders are not afraid of bold gestures; in fact the centralised French state has always revelled in daring and expensive *grands projets*. From the Ariane space rocket to the Grande Arche de la Défense and the Louvre pyramid, France has gone where other countries' finance ministers feared to tread, and despite any economic upsets, the country remains enduringly attractive to visitors.

HISTORY AND CULTURE

French history has been a constant quest for national identity: a conflict between strong regional loyalties and central authority. In around 2,000 BC, Celtic tribes – probably from eastern Europe – came looking for greener pastures in the areas that are now Franche-Comté, Alsace and Burgundy. At the same time, migrants from the Mediterranean countries were trickling into the south. The first recorded settlement was the trading post set up by Phocaean Greeks from Asia Minor at Massalia (Marseille) c.600 BC, followed by other ports at Hyères, Antibes and Nice. But the Greeks developed few contacts with the interior beyond a little commerce in olives and wine with the Celts of Burgundy. When their position was threatened by Ligurian pirates at sea and warlike tribes from inland, the merchants of Marseille called on Rome for help.

FROM GAUL TO FRANCE

In 125 BC, the Romans came in force, conquered the 'Gallic barbarians' and set up a fortress at Aquae Sextiae (Aix-en-Provence). They took

ASTÉRIX THE GAUL

In 1951 author René Goscinny met illustrator Albert Uderzo; eight years later they created the comic strip character Astérix the Gaul, the classic underdog, who gets his strength to fight the Romans from drinking a magic potion, for the launch of *Pilote* magazine. The first book came out in 1960, and since then an extraordinary 350 million have sold across the world, in languages from French to ancient Greek. There have even been film versions of the books. Goscinny died in 1977 and Uderzo hung up his pen in 2011. But productivity remains strong with their successors: 2006 saw the publication of the animated film *Astérix and the Vikings* and in 2014, *Astérix: The Land of the Gods* was released.

advantage of this new stronghold to create Provincia (now Provence), from the Alps to the Pyrénées, in order to guarantee communications between Italy and Spain. When this province was endangered by fresh attacks from the north, Julius Caesar himself took charge, conquering almost the whole of Gaul by 50 BC. Caesar drew Gaul's northeastern frontier at the Rhine, taking in present-day Belgium, and warned that the Germanic tribes

Pont du Gard aqueduct over the Gardon River

across the river – the Franks (after whom France is named), Alamans and Saxons – would threaten the security of the frontier.

The Romanisation of Gaul sent the most energetic warriors to defend the outposts of the empire, while their families settled down to work the land or build towns such as Lyon, Orange, Arles and Nîmes, and the first great highways between them. At the same time, merchants built up a thriving trade with the rest of the Roman Empire. The pattern for the peasantry and bourgeoisie of France was thus established.

Christianity was introduced into Gaul in the 1st century AD, but was not widely accepted until the late 4th century, when it became the empire's official religion. Large scale conversions were led by Martin de Tours, a soldier turned cleric (sword and cross were to form a regular alliance in French history). The new religion soon cemented national solidarity In the face of more barbarian invasions, this time by the Franks.

Gallic unity collapsed with the crumbling Roman Empire. King Clovis, the leader of the Franks, defeated the Roman armies at Soissons in 486 and won the allegiance of most Gallo-Romans by converting to Christianity 10 years later. With Paris as his capital, he extended his rule to the Mediterranean. The realm was divided up among his heirs and progressively fragmented by the rivalries of the Merovingian dynasty that battled for power over the next 300 years.

Despite this fragmentation, the Franks deeply impacted the cultural and linguistic heritage of France. The Germanic traditions and language of the north became distinct from the Gallo-Roman traditions longer preserved in the Mediterranean basin.

Spain's Arab rulers exploited this disunity to sweep north across Gaul, controlling Languedoc, Dordogne and a large part of Provence, before being defeated at Poitiers in 732 by the army of Charles Martel. Even the mighty Charlemagne, king of the Franks from 768 to 814, did not manage to create an enduring national unity; his sons fought for the spoils of his empire. The Normans from Scandinavia took advantage of the Carolingian dynasty's divided kingdom, pillaging their way inland along the Loire and the Seine, and plundering Paris in 845. In addition, Saracens invaded the Provençal coast from North Africa, and Magyar armies attacked Lorraine

Medieval fresco in Tour Ferrande, Provence

and Burgundy. To keep the support of the armies of the aristocracy, the kings had to give the former more and more land. Consequently, the realm broke up into the fiefdoms of the feudal Middle Ages, precursors of what are now the country's main provinces – Provence, Burgundy, Normandy, Brittany and so forth.

In the central region, from the Loire Valley to Belgium, Hugues Capet succeeded in achieving a precarious ascendancy and was crowned the first king of France in 987.

THE MIDDLE AGES

The alliance with the Church served as the underpinning of regal authority. In exchange for the anointment, the Church was enriched with lands and the right of taxation by tithe, a percentage of farmers' seasonal produce. After the more sober spirituality of the Romanesque churches, the soaring Gothic cathedrals of Chartres, Paris (Notre-Dame), Bourges and Amiens were at once monuments to the glory of God and testimony to the sheer power, spiritual and temporal, of the Roman Catholic Church.

A chivalrous tale

The *Chanson de Roland* is an epic poem about the death of one of Charlemagne's brave knights, who was commanding his army when its rearguard was crushed by the Basques in the Pyrénées in 778. The work launched the idea of chivalrous self-sacrifice for France.

France, dubbed by the pope the 'eldest daughter of the Church', took the lead in the Crusades against the 'infidels' in Palestine, stopping off on the way across Europe to massacre heretics and infidels themselves. Louis IX of France, lauded as the ultimate Christian king for the justice he handed down to his subjects and for the Crusades he led to the Holy Land, was sainted after his death in Tunis in 1270. From 1309 to 1377, Avignon was the papal seat.

France had another major preoccupation: England. In 1066 Duc Guillaume of Normandy crossed the English Channel in a successful military campaign and became William the Conqueror. For the next 400 years, English and French monarchs fought over the sovereignty of various parts of France, including Aquitaine, Flanders, Normandy and Touraine. The two countries engaged in tangled marital alliances and military clashes more important to national morale than to resolving their perennial conflict – such as Bouvines (1214), a victory for the French, and Crécy (1346) and Agincourt (1415), victories for the English. Finally, a teenager from Lorraine, Jeanne d'Arc (Joan of Arc), roused the French to resist the English at Orléans. The English captured her and burned her at the stake in Rouen in 1431, but her martyrdom stirred national pride sufficiently to oust the English from France 20 years later.

The disputes among nobles were not the first concern of ordinary French citizens. To the common man, wars were just another hardship, taking sons away from the farm to fight, while the armies – French as much as foreign – ravaged the land or pillaged the towns. During war and peace alike in this feudal age, the Church and the aristocracy continued to claim their respective portions of the peasants' labour, leaving barely enough for subsistence. All too frequently a cycle of drought, famine and plague would decimate the population.

In any case, large portions of France were independently controlled by powerful dukes whose allegiance to the king was only nominal. The modern unity of France was in the making.

THE ANCIEN RÉGIME

Absolute power was the dominant feature of what post-Revolutionary France called the *Ancien Régime*. The monarchy made noticeable gains under François I (1515–47). He strengthened central administration and abandoned an initially tolerant policy toward the Protestants. A debonair Renaissance prince and patron of the arts, he introduced a grandiose style at court and commissioned the building of Fontainebleau. In foreign affairs, after he had crushed the Duke of Milan's army at Marignano and formed a showy alliance with Henry VIII of England, François I's European ambitions were halted by the German Emperor, Charles V. François even suffered the indignity of a year's imprisonment in Madrid, following a resounding defeat at Pavia in 1525.

The bloody 16th-century conflicts between Catholics and Protestants throughout Europe centred more on political and financial intrigue than on questions of theology. The French Wars of Religion pitted the Catholic forces of the regent Catherine de Médicis against the Protestant (Huguenot) camp headed by Henri de Navarre. Their crisis came on 24 August 1572 with the infamous St Bartholomew's Day Massacre. Two thousand Protestants, in Paris for Henri's wedding to Catherine's daughter Marguerite de Valois, were killed. The general massacre of Protestants spread to the countryside, and by October another 30,000 had lost their lives.

The conciliatory policies that painfully emerged after the bloodshed brought the Protestant Prince of Navarre to the throne as Henri IV (1589–1610), but not before he promised to convert to Catholicism. The enormous personal popularity of this good natured

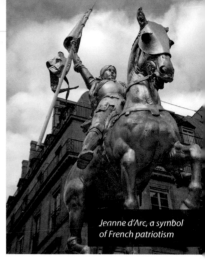

Jeanne d'Arc, a symbol of French patriotism

but tough king from the Pyrénées proved vital for healing the wounds from the bitter wars. The Edict of Nantes was signed in 1598 to protect the Protestants, and five years later the Jesuits were allowed back into France. Henri maintained his reputation as a worthy and brave leader – and at the same time as an incorrigible womaniser – until his assassination in 1610 by a religious zealot.

The country floundered in uncertainty under the regency of Marie de Médicis, mother of the young Louis XIII, until Cardinal Richelieu took charge as prime minister in 1624. Directing national policy until his death in 1642, Richelieu reasserted the authority of his king against both the conservative Catholics who surrounded the queen mother and the Protestant forces that were fiercely defending the privileges granted them by the Edict of Nantes. With his successful siege of the Protestant stronghold at La Rochelle, the cardinal neutralised the threat of their military strength while still guaranteeing their freedom of worship.

Richelieu's major achievement was the increased centralisation of royal power, laying the foundations for the strong sense of national identity that has characterised France ever since. He tightened the king's control over legislation and taxes, enraging the Vatican by daring to impose a new levy on the Church. More powerful royal stewards were sent out to diminish the autonomy of the regional *parlements*, councils with judicial rather than legislative functions, dominated by the high clergy and the nobles. The cardinal also established the Académie Française in 1635 to ensure the purity and clarity of the French language through its *Dictionnaire* and *Grammaire*.

Promoting overseas trade and the founding of a navy, Richelieu launched France on the road to empire with the colonisation of Guadeloupe and Martinique in the Caribbean. In Europe, the Catholic cardinal, master of practical politics, was not above supporting the Protestant Swedish, Danish, and German forces in the Thirty Years' War against the Catholic Austrians, Italians and Spanish. All that mattered was that it served France's interests.

Richelieu's protégé, Mazarin, another cardinal, took over the job of prime minister during the minority of Louis XIV. The court and regional

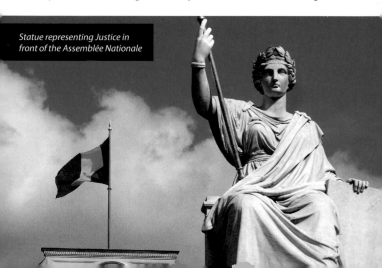

Statue representing Justice in front of the Assemblée Nationale

aristocracy were infuriated by the Italian-born churchman's intimate relationship with the king's mother, Anne of Austria. Nor did they like his astounding knack for amassing a vast personal fortune while managing, very efficiently, the affairs of state. But most of all, they despised the way in which he eroded the nobles' power and smoothed the path to an increasingly absolutist monarchy.

The revolts of the *Fronde* forced Mazarin, Anne and the boy king to flee from Paris in 1649. But the royal family's triumphant return three years later, with the rebellious nobles crushed, saw the monarchy stronger and more entrenched than ever.

THE SUN KING

Louis XIV drew his own conclusions from Mazarin's careful coaching in the affairs of state. When he began his personal rule in 1661, at the age of 23, there was no question of a new prime minister impinging on the royal prerogative. Adopting the unequivocal emblem of the sun, Louis was to be outshone by no-one. Counsellors were wholly subservient. Louis never called upon the parliamentary assembly of the *Etats généraux*. He moved the court to his hunting lodge at Versailles, impoverished the nobility by forcing them to contribute to the vast luxury of his palace, and imposed as their sole function the support of the king in time of war.

Versailles was the shining star of Europe by its architectural splendour and the hypnotic power of Louis XIV's cult of selfglorification. In his lifetime, many petty European princes tried to imitate Louis's style with their own little Versailles, complete with court artists and sycophants. But Versailles was not without cost. It took French historians a long time to come to terms with the less attractive realities of what Louis's style cost the nation.

To enhance his glory, the Sun King turned to foreign conquest. The devastating military expedition he launched across the Rhineland and Palatinate, and the series of largely fruitless wars with Spain, Holland, England and Sweden did not endear him to the European people. Moreover, these ventures left France's once-thriving economy in ruins.

Molière

Jean-Baptiste Poquelin (1622–73), better known as Molière, remains France's most acclaimed writer of comic drama. His often stereotypical protagonists highlight such human failings as hypocrisy, greed and miserliness. Molière acted in many of his own works and famously collapsed on stage during a performance of *The Imaginary Invalid*. The audience tragically believed his histrionics to be part of the act; he died soon afterwards.

At home, his authoritarian rule required a brutal police force. Taxes soared to pay for his wars, and a growing number of peasants had to abandon their fields when press-ganged into his armies. Influenced in later life by the Catholic piety of Madame de Maintenon, his mistress and subsequently secret wife, Louis put an end to religious freedom for Protestants by revoking the Edict of Nantes. In the face of forced conversions, the Protestant Huguenots – many of them the most talented bankers, merchants, and artisans of their generation – fled to Switzerland, Germany, Holland, England and Scandinavia.

Louis died in 1715. Having outlived his children and grandchildren, he was succeeded by his five-year-old great-grandson, Louis XV. But government was in the hands of the late king's cultured, libertine and atheist brother, Philippe d'Orléans.

After the morose twilight years of the Sun King, the societal tone changed with the satiric pen of Voltaire and the erotic fantasies of Watteau's paintings and Marivaux's comedies. The court moved back from Versailles to Paris. The generally lazy regent gave incompetent nobles too much of a say in the running of the state. Regional *parlements* obtained the right to make protest, and the monarchy gradually weakened.

The easy-going Louis XV was called the *Bien-Aimé* (Beloved), at least in the first half of his reign. The king seemed more interested in his mistresses than in running a tight ship of state. Despite this (or perhaps because of it), the economy recovered and the middle classes strengthened. The overseas empire expanded in the East and West Indies, and arts and letters flourished in this age of enlightenment.

But the new voices were a clear threat to the established order. Diderot's *Encyclopédie* championed reason over traditional religion; Rousseau discoursed on the origins of inequality; Voltaire took literary pot shots at the fattening hypocrites of the ruling class in France.

THE REVOLUTION

Louis XVI, grandson of Louis XV, found himself attacked on all sides. The stubborn aristocracy and high clergy were anxious to protect their ancient privileges; a burgeoning bourgeoisie longed for reforms that would give them greater opportunity; the peasantry was no longer prepared to bear the burden of feudal extortion; and a growing urban populace of artisans groaned under intolerable hardships.

The *Etats généraux* convened for the first time in 175 years. It was clearly the king's enduring absolutism rather than the throne itself that

Versailles reflects Louis XIV's talent for self-glorification

was under fire. For reactionary nobles, the king was the guarantor of their hereditary status. Liberal reformers wanted a constitutional monarchy similar to England's, not a republic. Even the grievances drawn up by the peasants and townspeople insisted on continuing devotion to the king.

Two months later, the blindness of the king's conservative advisors and his own weakness and vacillation led to the explosion of centuries of frustration and rage – which culminated in the storming of the Bastille, the prison-fortress in Paris. On that fateful day, 14 July 1789, the king went hunting near his château at Versailles. At the end of the day, Louis – apparently oblivious to events in Paris – wrote in his diary, *'Rien'* ('Nothing').

A National Assembly voted a charter for liberty and equality, the great *Declaration of the Rights of Man and of the Citizen*. The aristocracy's feudal rights were abolished, the Church's massive land-holdings confiscated and sold off. Rather than compromise, the king fled Paris in a vain effort to join up with armed forces hostile to the Revolution. With Austrian and German armies massing on France's frontiers and the forces of counter-revolution gathering inside the country, the militant revolutionary Jacobins led by Maximilien de Robespierre saw the king's flight as the ultimate betrayal. A Republic was declared in 1792, and Louis XVI was guillotined in 1793. His son Louis XVII died in obscure circumstances under the Revolutionary government, probably in 1795.

MADAME LA GUILLOTINE

On the northern side of the place de la Concorde, Paris, where the Statue of the City of Brest is today, Louis XVI was executed on 21 January 1793. Later, the guillotine was shifted to the entrance to the Tuileries. According to official estimates, 1,119 people were decapitated here including Charlotte Corday, the Girondist leader, Queen Marie-Antoinette, Prince Philippe, Madame Dubarry, the poet André Chénier and Robespierre.

Eugène Delacroix's Liberty Leading the People

Under pressure from the poorer classes, who did not want the Revolution appropriated for the exclusive benefit of the bourgeoisie, the Jacobin-led revolutionary committee ordered sweeping measures of economic and social reform, which were accompanied by a wave of mass executions, known as the Terror, aimed at moderates as well as aristocrats. Despite his attempts to quell the extremists, Robespierre was overthrown and guillotined in the counterattack of the propertied classes.

NAPOLEON BONAPARTE

During their *Directoire,* a new wave of executions – the White (royalist) Terror – decimated the Jacobins and their supporters. But the bourgeoisie, fearing both the royalists and their foreign backers, turned for salvation to a Corsican soldier triumphantly campaigning against the Revolution's foreign enemies – Napoleon Bonaparte.

In between defeating the Austrians in Italy and a less successful campaign against the British in Egypt, in 1795 Bonaparte returned to Paris to crush the royalists, and four years later he staged a coup against the *Directoire.* He was just 30 years old.

In the first flush of dictatorship as First Consul, he established the Banque de France, created state-run *lycées* (high schools), and gave the country its first national set of laws, the *Code Napoléon*. The centralisation dear to Richelieu and Louis XIV was becoming a reality.

The supreme self-made man, Bonaparte in 1804 became Emperor Napoleon at a coronation ceremony in which he audaciously took the crown of golden laurels from the pope and placed it on his own head. He managed to simultaneously pursue foreign conquests in Germany and Austria and domestic reforms that included a modernised university, a police force, and proper supplies of drinking water for Parisians. During his disastrous campaign in Russia, he found time in Moscow to draw up a new statute for the *Comédie-Française* (the national theatre), which had been dissolved during the Revolution.

The nationalism that Napoleon invoked in his conquest of Europe's *Ancien Régime* turned against him in Spain, Russia and Germany. The monarchies regrouped to force him from power in 1814. Nevertheless, he made a brilliant but brief comeback the following year – before an alliance of British, Prussian, Belgian and Dutch troops inflicted the final defeat at Waterloo.

Napoleon Bonaparte

TOWARDS DEMOCRACY

At the end of the Napoleonic era, the monarchy was restored. The new king, Louis XVIII, tried at first to reconcile the restored monarchy with the reforms of the Revolution and Napoleon's empire. But his nobles were intent on revenge and imposed a second, even more violent,

White Terror against Jacobins and Bonapartists, including some of Napoleon's greatest generals.

Louis's reactionary successor, his brother Charles X, was interested only in renewing the traditions of the *Ancien Régime,* even having himself anointed and crowned at the ancient cathedral of Reims. But the middle classes were no longer prepared to tolerate the restraints on their freedom, nor the worsening condition of the economy in the hands of an incompetent aristocracy. They reasserted their rights in the insurrection of July 1830 – the kind of liberal revolution they would have preferred back in 1789 – paving the way for the 'bourgeois monarchy' of Louis-Philippe.

This last king of France, heir of the progressive Orléans branch of the royal family, encouraged the country's exploitation of the Industrial Revolution and the complementary extension of its overseas empire in Asia and Africa (Algeria had been occupied just before the 1830 revolution). But the new factories created an urban working class clamouring for improvement of its miserable working and living conditions. The regime's response of ferocious repression plus numerous other ineptitudes led to a third revolution in 1848, with the Bonapartists, led by Napoleon's nephew, emerging triumphant.

The Second Republic ended four years later when the man whom Victor Hugo called 'Napoléon le Petit' staged a coup to become Emperor Napoleon III. Determined to cloak himself in the legend of his uncle's grandeur, Louis Napoleon saw his own role as that of champion of the people. But he used harsh anti-press laws and loyalty oaths to quell the libertarian spirit that had brought him to power.

France's economy flourished thanks to the expansion of a vigorous entrepreneurial capitalism in iron, steel and railways, augmented by overseas ventures such as the Suez Canal. Despite the emperor's obsession with the new 'Red Peril' – Marx and Engels' 1848 *Communist Manifesto,* which was being circulated in Paris – he could not prevent such social reforms as the workers' right to form unions and even to strike.

With the excessive enthusiasm that characterised the age, Baron Haussmann's urban planning *(see box)* redeveloped old Parisian neighbourhoods and the architect Viollet-le-Duc restored some of France's Gothic cathedrals and medieval châteaux. Victor Hugo, in exile in Guernsey, was writing *Les Misérables,* while Baudelaire was working on *Les Fleurs du Mal,* and Offenbach was composing operettas such as *La Belle Hélène.* Courbet was painting his vast canvases of provincial life, and Manet his then highly controversial *Déjeuner sur l'Herbe.*

Society was optimistic. The bourgeoisie showed off its newfound prosperity with extravagant furnishings, silks, satins and baubles, and in 1852 Paris opened its first department store, Au Bon Marché. France was developing a strong national identity as provider of culture for Europe, as well as a high level of social critique and constant pressure for improvement.

However, Germany had an account to settle. In 1870, Prussian Chancellor Bismarck exploited an obscure diplomatic conflict with France to unite the various German principalities and kingdoms into a fighting force well equipped for war. After a lightning victory over the illprepared French armies, the Germans marched on Paris and laid siege to the city, which finally capitulated in January 1871 in the face of dwindling food supplies. As part of the settlement ending the war, Alsace and a portion of Lorraine were ceded to Germany.

THE THIRD REPUBLIC

Defeat shattered the Second Empire. While the new Third Republic's government under Adolphe Thiers negotiated the

Parisian planning

The layout of contemporary Paris owes much to Napoleon III's chief town planner, the Prefect Baron Georges-Eugène Haussmann (1809–91), who was responsible for reorganising Paris in the late 19th century. He gutted and boldly rebuilt the centre, installing new water mains and a sewerage system, and replaced narrow medieval roads with a network of wide boulevards *(the grands boulevards),* which improved traffic flow and made crowd control easier.

terms of surrender, the workers' communes refused to give in. In March 1871 they took over Paris and a few provincial cities, and held out for 10 weeks. In the end they were brutally crushed by government troops, and order was restored.

France resumed its industrial progress, quickly paid off its enormous war-reparations debt to Germany, and expanded its overseas empire in Africa and Indochina. Rediscovered national pride found its perfect expression in the Eiffel Tower, thrust into the Paris skies for the Universal Exhibition of 1889.

In 1874 the first exhibition of Impressionism had blown away the dust and cobwebs of the artistic establishment. Novelist Emile Zola poured forth arguments against industrial exploitation. Rodin, more restrained, sculpted masterpieces such as *Le Penseur* (The Thinker). Leading the 'republican' hostility to the Church's entrenched position in the schools, in 1882 Jules Ferry enacted the legislation that has formed the basis of France's formidable state education system ever since.

On the right, nationalist forces were motivated by a desire to hit back at Germany, seeing all contact with foreigners or any form of 'cosmopolitanism' as a threat to the nation's honour and integrity. For many, the Jews were the embodiment of this threat – Edouard Drumont's vehemently anti-Semitic *La France Juive* (Jewish France) was a runaway national bestseller. It appeared in 1886, eight years before Captain Alfred Dreyfus, an Alsatian Jew in the French Army, was arrested on what proved to be trumped-up charges of spying for the Germans. In a case that pitted the fragile honour of the Army against the very survival of French republican democracy, the captain had to wait over 12 years for full rehabilitation.

The desire for revenge against Germany remained. And as Germany's own imperial ambitions grew, competition for world markets became intense. Most of France went enthusiastically into World War I, and came out of it victorious yet bled white. With the 1919 Treaty of Versailles, France recovered Alsace and Lorraine; but 1,350,000 men had been lost in the four years of fighting. The national economy was shattered, and political divisions were more extreme than ever.

In face of the fears aroused by the Russian Revolution of 1917, the conservative parties dominated the immediate post-war period, while a new French Communist Party, loyal to Moscow, split with the Socialists in 1920. France seemed less aware of the threat from Nazi Germany, allowing Hitler to remilitarise the Rhineland in 1936 in breach of the Versailles Treaty, a step Hitler later said he had never dreamed of getting away with.

In the 1930s, extreme right-wing groups such as Action Française and Croix-de-Feu (Cross of Fire) provided a strong antidemocratic undercurrent to the political turmoil of financial scandal and parliamentary corruption. The bloody 1934 riots on place de la Concorde in Paris offered a disturbing echo to the street fighting in Fascist Italy and Nazi Germany.

The left-wing parties responded by banding together in a Popular Front, which the Socialists led to power in 1936. Within the first few weeks, Léon Blum's government nationalised the railways, brought in a 40-hour week, and instituted the workers' first holidays with pay. But the Communists broke the alliance after Blum first failed to support the Republicans in the Spanish Civil War and then – faced with financial difficulties – put a brake on the reforms.

WAR AND PEACE

Blum's government collapsed in 1938, and the new prime minister, Edouard Daladier, negotiated the Munich agreements with Hitler, Mussolini and Britain's Neville Chamberlain. A year later, France was once again at war with Germany.

Relying on the defensive strategy of the fortified Maginot Line along the northeast frontier with Germany (but not facing Belgium), the French were unprepared for the German invasion across the Ardennes in May 1940. With fast tanks and superior air power, the Germans reached Paris 30 days later. Marshal Philippe Pétain, the hero of World War I, capitulated on behalf of the French on June 16. Two days later, on BBC radio's French service from London, General de Gaulle appealed for national resistance.

Compared with other occupied countries such as Belgium, Holland and Denmark, France's collaboration with the Germans is a rather inglorious story. Based in the Auvergnat spa town of Vichy, the French government often proved more zealous than its masters in suppressing

Erecting Paris's most iconic landmark, the Eiffel Tower

General Charles de Gaulle

civil liberties and drawing up anti-Jewish legislation. It was French police who rounded up the deportees for the concentration camps, many of them denounced by French civilians seeking to profit from the confiscation of property. The fighters of the underground Resistance movement were heroic, but they were a tiny minority, a few of them conservative patriots such as de Gaulle, most of them socialists and communists, and also a handful of refugees from Eastern Europe.

Deliverance came when the Allies landed on the beaches of Normandy on D-Day (6 June 1944). De Gaulle, with his canny sense of history, took a major step towards rebuilding national self-confidence by insisting that French armed forces fight with the Americans and British for the liberation of the country, but, above all, that the French army be the first to enter Paris itself.

After the high emotion of de Gaulle's march down the Champs-Elysées, the business of post-war reconstruction, though boosted by the Americans' Marshall Plan, proved arduous; the wartime alliance of de Gaulle's conservatives and the Communist Party soon broke down. The general could not stand the political squabbles of the Fourth Republic and withdrew from public life. Governments changed repeatedly, but the French muddled through, and intellectuals debated the existentialist merit of writer/philosophers Albert Camus and Jean-Paul Sartre in Paris's Left Bank cafés.

The French empire was collapsing. After France's fruitless last stand in Vietnam, Pierre Mendès-France wisely negotiated an Indo-Chinese peace settlement. He handed Pondicherry over to India and gave Tunisia its independence, but was ousted from office as hostilities broke out in Algeria.

De Gaulle returned from the wilderness in 1958, ostensibly to keep Algeria French. But he'd seen the writing on the wall and brought the war to an end with Algerian independence in 1962. His major task was to rescue France from the chaos of the Fourth Republic. The new constitution, tailor-made to de Gaulle's authoritarian requirements, placed the president above parliament, where he could pursue his own policies outside the messy arena of party politics. However, the colonial struggles in Algeria and Morocco were to have a significant impact on French national identity in later years. As the empire receded, colonised populations from North and Central Africa, Indochina and elsewhere began to move to France and alter the French identity once more.

De Gaulle's visions of grandeur and of a country independent of NATO and the Warsaw Pact gave France a renewed self-confidence. One of his great achievements was a close alliance with West Germany, overcoming centuries of bloodshed between the two peoples.

MAY 1968

In the month of May 1968, a general feeling of malaise erupted into aggressive demonstrations against the Vietnam War, government control of the media and the stagnant values of the older generation. The tension increased when the students removed paving stones in the Latin Quarter, built barricades and occupied the Sorbonne. Joined by the workers of the left, the student demonstrations escalated into a national crisis. Shaken badly by these events and by his failing foreign and economic policy, de Gaulle relinquished power to his former prime minister Georges Pompidou in 1969. Later known chiefly for the cultural centre at Beaubourg bearing his name, Pompidou died after a long illness in 1974.

THE PRESIDENTS

In the ensuing presidential election, Gaullist Valéry Giscard d'Estaing beat socialist François Mitterrand. Despite his right-wing tendencies,

Giscard d'Estaing's seven-year presidency incorporated reforms desired by the left: less restrictive divorce laws, legalised abortion, widely available contraception and a voting age of 18. Although an élitist patrician, Giscard d'Estaing was also a modernist and technocrat with an international outlook.

In 1981 Mitterrand defeated Giscard d'Estaing, bringing the left to power for the first time under the Fifth Republic. Like Giscard d'Estaing, Mitterrand surprised those unfamiliar with French politics by maintaining close ties with the US and advocating only limited nationalisation of French industry. As the longest-serving president in French history, he played a significant role on the world stage. In foreign policy, he cemented the Franco-German axis at the heart of the European Union.

INTO THE 21ST CENTURY

Despite the differences between De Gaulle, Pompidou, Giscard and Mitterrand, France continued to function in much the same way along

1968 student riots

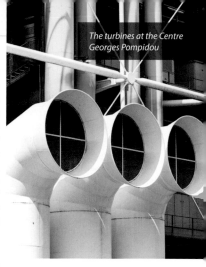
The turbines at the Centre Georges Pompidou

several fronts: the government continued to develop its independent military strike force and forge its own distinctive foreign policy. In 1989 France celebrated the bicentennial of the Revolution, which led to an orgy of self-congratulation and analysis. It was a heady era that ended with the election of the former Mayor of Paris, the right-wing Jacques Chirac, as president in 1995. By the end of the 20th century the French economy was improving again, unemployment had fallen and a 35-hour week had been introduced.

The victory of the left in 1997 brought about a period of cohabitation between the right-wing president, Chirac, and the left-wing government of Lionel Jospin. This ended in 2002 with Jospin's resignation. Chirac was re-elected and centre-right Jean-Pierre Raffarin became prime minister heading a coalition government.

By the end of Chirac's second term, however, there was a widespread feeling that the previous 14 years had been a time of squandered opportunities. Social divisions, racial tensions, high unemployment and corruption scandals brought calls for radical change. In the 2007 presidential election, the country voted for the tough modernisation policies of centre-right Nicolas Sarkozy. By late 2008, in response to the global financial crisis he was a leading figure, along with Germany's Chancellor Angela Merkel, in creating the G20 summits of world economies. By 2009 the Eurozone crisis was plunging Europe's economies into debt and Sarkozy was once again in the forefront of discussions. In January 2012 France, formerly one of the strongest of Europe's economies, had its AAA credit rating removed. Sarkozy's popularity was waning and he was narrowly beaten by Socialist François Hollande in the 2012 elections.

In 2013, Hollande approved same-sex marriages, making France the 13th country in the world to do so. In 2015, France became a victim of terrorism as the so-called Islamic State carried out a series of co-ordinated terror attacks in Paris, killing 142 innocent people in the process. Hollande swiftly responded by authorising a series of airstrikes on terrorist strong-holds throughout Syria. Hollande has also attempted to control the global refugee crisis, many of whom enter France illegally on their way to the United Kingdom. In 2017, Hollande was replaced by Emmanuel Macron, a former minister for the economy, pro-EU centrist and France's youngest president. He promised to defend Europe and create unity in a fractured France and. in 2022, having led the country through the Covid pandemic, gained a majority for a second term, his nearest rival being nationalist-popularist Marine Le Pen. His second term sees him attempt to navigate rising inflation in France due to fallout from the war in Ukraine.

President Emmanuel Macron

HISTORICAL LANDMARKS

28,000 BC Cro-Magnon man in Dordogne.

2000 BC Celts invade France from east.

125–121 BC Romans establish colony of Provincia (Provence).

59–50 BC Julius Caesar conquers Gaul.

AD 486 'Barbarians' end Roman control.

768–814 Charlemagne, king of the Franks.

987 Hugues Capet, first king of France.

1066 Duke William of Normandy conquers England.

1337–1453 Hundred Years' War.

1431 Joan of Arc executed.

1624–42 Cardinal Richelieu governs for Louis XIII.

1661–1715 Louis XIV moves court to Versailles.

1789 French Revolution. Fall of the Bastille (July 14).

1804 Bonaparte crowns himself Emperor Napoleon.

1815 Napoleon defeated at Waterloo, Louis XVIII restored to throne.

1848 Liberal Revolution overthrows monarchy.

1870–1 Franco-Prussian War. Germans seize Alsace-Lorraine.

1914–18 World War I.

1939–45 World War II. Germany occupies France.

1944 Allies invade Normandy (June 6).

1945–6 De Gaulle heads the Fourth Republic's first government.

1958–69 De Gaulle is first president of the new Fifth Republic.

1968 Student rebels shake government.

1981 Mitterrand elected Fifth Republic's first Socialist president.

2002 The euro becomes France's official currency. Chirac is re-elected.

2007 Nicolas Sarkozy is elected president.

2008–2012 France is hit by world recession and the Euro crisis.

2012 François Hollande elected president in May.

2015 Twelve people are killed in a terrorist attack on the HQ of the *Charlie Hebdo* satirical magazine in Paris, the so-called Islamic State claims responsibility.

2016 Bastille Day terrorist attack in Nice kills 86 and injures hundreds.

2017 Emmanuel Macron elected as France's youngest ever president in May.

2023 France hosts the Rugby World Cup in September.

The old town in Hyères, Côte d'Azur

OUT AND ABOUT

France is a large country of infinite variety, so a great many factors come into play as you decide which parts to visit. Do you want to see historic sights and tour museums and art galleries? Do you want to lie on beaches or hike in mountains? Do you want to drive or use public transport? To make the geography (if not the choice) simpler, we've divided the country into five regions: Paris and its vicinity; the Northeast; the Northwest; the Southeast; and the Southwest. Depending on how much time you have, you may want to combine two or three of these regions in order to get a sense of the great diversity of French life: Paris and the wine country; the mountains; or the Atlantic and Mediterranean coasts.

However, the mix doesn't have to be simply geographic. France's cathedrals, museums and palaces deserve your attention, but a holiday incorporating visits to them may combine well with country walks or time at the beach. And if you feel like being idle, France has many pretty backwaters, where it's a simple joy to do absolutely nothing.

Many people do not have the option of going to France outside the main holiday periods – Easter, July and August. But if it's at all possible, plan your visit for the spring, autumn or even the winter, when sightseeing destinations are less crowded.

You may have more opportunity to meet the French themselves out of holiday season. In

Admission fees

The majority of museums and galleries in France charge an admission fee; hence we have not specified this in individual listings. The fee may vary according to visitor age and inclusion of any special exhibitions. There are security checks at entrances to major attractions. Suitcases and large travel bags are not permitted in many museums, nor can they be left in the cloakroom.

August many Parisians leave the city, for example, and a large number of shops and businesses close, making it almost seem as if the city's visitors outnumber the locals.

PARIS

Paris ❶ has been described as a city-state in its own right, so different is it from the rest of the country. The capital and its immediate surroundings remain a magnet for artists, tourists, students, businessmen – in short, everyone except perhaps the farmer and fisherman, who may well head there solely to protest at government policies. A vibrant city, Paris sets tastes and fashions for France and the world. For years, ambitious French people saw Paris as the only place to make their fortune, so every region of France, along with its local cuisine, is represented in the metropolis. Renewed pride in France's provincial cities is reducing this trend, but Paris retains its aura of superiority.

The skyline at dusk

Before Paris became the national capital, it was the home of the medieval dukes of the region known as the Ile-de-France – which, by gradually asserting itself over other duchies such as Burgundy and Normandy, imposed its name on the whole country. The Paris basin is a treasury of national monuments. Roughly bounded by four rivers – the Seine, Oise, Aisne and Marne – the Ile-de-France was the birthplace of the first great Gothic cathedrals, including St-Denis, Senlis, Chartres and Beauvais. It was the cradle of the French monarchy and its surrounding greenery and dense forests also provided good sites for later kings and nobles to build their châteaux, well away from the troublesome mob of Paris, at Fontainebleau, Chantilly and Versailles. All of the interesting sights around the capital make for an easy day trip by car or local train, enabling you to keep your Paris base if you wish, although you may enjoy a change of scene and find the local country inns less expensive.

The city and people of Paris share a boundless self-confidence, which exudes from its grandiose monuments and museums, its bistros, boutiques and beautiful broad boulevards; the same air of self-confidence is given off by many of the city's residents, from the local *boulanger* to that most stereotypical of Parisian characters, the irate motorist.

You'll readily forgive the bombast of some of the monumental architecture when you see what makes this the City of Light. Stand on the Pont Royal in late afternoon and look down the Seine to the glass-panelled Grand Palais, bathed in the pink-and-blue glow of the river. This unique light brings a phosphorescence to the most commonplace little square or side street.

The Right Bank still conjures up an image of solid bourgeois respectability. Historically the stronghold of merchants and royalty, today it remains the home of commerce and government. Faubourg St-Honoré offers the luxury of jewellery shops and haute couture; the Champs-Elysées claims the first-run cinemas, airline companies and car showrooms.

In contrast, the Left Bank has always presented a bohemian and intellectual image, dating back to the founding of the university and monasteries;

today, the Sorbonne, the Académie Française, the publishing houses and the myriad bookshops continue to exercise an intellectual magnetism.

An unceasing flow and interchange of citizenry from one bank to the other takes place across the bridges of the Seine. But despite these migrations, time seems to stand still in many Paris neighbourhoods. Areas may go in and out of fashion but each retains its particular sense of identity.

THE SEINE

Cutting through Paris, the Seine is a spectacular vantage point for many of the city's great landmarks. Despite the roar of the traffic on the main roads adjacent to it, it's also a wonderful place for a quiet stroll.

A guided boat trip is a good introduction to the city, displaying in leisurely fashion sights including the Eiffel Tower, the Palais de Chaillot and Trocadéro Gardens, the Grand and Petit Palais, the Palais Bourbon, the Louvre and Notre-Dame. Look out for the following bridges en route:

Pont-Neuf (*neuf* means 'new') is in fact Paris's oldest standing bridge, completed by Henri IV in 1606. It straddles the Ile de la Cité, and was initially populated with street-singers, charlatans, prostitutes, pickpockets and bouquinistes selling books and pamphlets out of boxes. Established booksellers on the island were enraged and drove the bouquinistes off to the banks of the river, where they've been ever since.

The **Pont Royal**, built for Louis XIV in 1685–9, commands views of the Louvre and Tuileries on the Right Bank, the Musée d'Orsay on the Left, the Grand and Petit Palais downriver and the Institut de France upstream.

The **Pont de la Concorde**, the bridge of the French Revolution, was erected between 1787 and 1791. Stones from the demolished Bastille prison were used for its support structure – galling for Royalists, since the bridge had originally been named Pont Louis XVI.

The **Pont Alexandre III** is undoubtedly the most romantic with its Belle Epoque lanterns and melodramatic statues of Fame and Pegasus.

Paris is one of the world's most densely populated capitals and remains a living city, unchilled by a dearth of city-centre residents. Its non-stop street scene derives from the fact that nearly every one of its 20 *arrondissements* (districts) has shops, offices and apartments side by side and on top of each other. Get out and explore the streets, the open markets and the cafés. You will find that each *quartier* has its own personality and something special to offer.

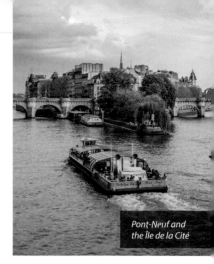

Pont-Neuf and
the Île de la Cité

THE ISLANDS

In the 3rd century BC, the Celtic tribe of the Parisii built their first huts on the Ile de la Cité, the largest island in the Seine. In 52 BC, Roman legions conquered the settlement and founded Lutetia Parisiorum on the left bank. During the Middle Ages, the island was the centre of political, religious and judicial power, not only for Paris but for the whole of France. Nowadays, the island is the geographical centre of the capital and home to several of the city's main official buildings – the Conciergerie, the law courts, the police headquarters (home to the fictional detective Maigret) and the Hôtel-Dieu hospital. The churches of Sainte-Chapelle and the gothic behemoth Notre-Dame make the island the focal point for religious tourism in the city.

Ile de la Cité

Shaped like a boat, with the pretty square du Vert-Galant as its prow, the Ile de la Cité is the ancient heart of Paris, settled by the Celtic 'Parisii' people as early as the 3rd century BC. In the middle of the 19th century, it fell victim to the urban planning of Baron Haussmann. The much-praised but often insensitive prefect of Paris swept away most of the medieval and 17th-century structures, leaving only place Dauphine and rue Chanoinesse as testimony to the island's rich residential life.

The baron also seriously considered replacing the triangular **place Dauphine**'s gracious gabled-and-arcaded architecture with neo-Grecian colonnades – but was forced out of office before the demolishers could move in. Built in 1607 by Henri IV, whose equestrian statue can be seen on the nearby Pont-Neuf, the square's tree-lined pavement cafés are a world away from the roar of the city.

On boulevard du Palais the massive **Palais de Justice** (Mon–Fri 8.30am–6.30pm), housing the law courts of modern Paris, holds echoes of the nation's earliest kings, who dwelt here, and of the aristocrats and revolutionary leaders who in turn were imprisoned here before their execution.

The building also conceals a Gothic masterpiece: **Sainte-Chapelle** Ⓐ

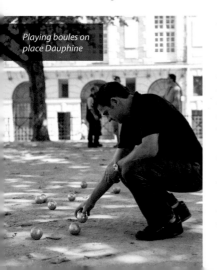

Playing boules on place Dauphine

(www.sainte-chapelle.fr; daily Apr–Sep 9.30am–6pm, Wed until 9.30pm, Oct–Mar 9am–5pm). The chapel's harmonious proportions and soaring walls dominated by exquisite 13th-century stained glass (the oldest in Paris) give it an ethereal quality, in startling contrast to the ponderous palace surrounding it. It was completed during the 13th century by King Louis IX (later St-Louis) to house a number of precious relics such as Christ's crown of thorns. The 15 **stained-glass windows** depict 1,134 scenes from the Bible. Between 1789 and 1815 the chapel served variously as a flour warehouse, a clubhouse for high-ranking dandies and an archive for Bonaparte's Consulate.

As a sinister prison, the **Conciergerie** (www.paris-conciergerie. fr; daily 9.30am–6pm), named after the royally appointed *concierge* in charge of common-law criminals, welcomed Marie-Antoinette, Robespierre, Madame du Barry, Danton and 2,500 others into its 'ante-chamber of the guillotine'. The Salle des Girondins displays a guillotine blade, the crucifix to which Marie-Antoinette prayed before execution and the lock of Robespierre's cell. Look down on the Cour des Femmes, where husbands, lovers, wives and mistresses were allowed one last tryst before the tumbrels arrived to take them on their final journey.

The great cathedral of **Notre-Dame de Paris** Ⓑ (www.notredame deparis.fr) was engulfed in flames on 15th April 2019, with the spire destroyed and the roof gutted. The restoration is on track to be completed in 2024 but parts, including the archaeological crypt and the parvis, are already open. Check the website for the latest information. Extensive landscaping plans to revamp the space around it are also underway and are due to be completed in 2027.

The site has held religious significance for over two millennia. In Roman times a temple to Jupiter stood here, followed in the 4th century by the first Christian church, St-Etienne. A second church, dedicated to the Virgin, joined it 200 years later. Both were left derelict by Norman invaders, and Bishop Maurice de Sully authorised construction of a cathedral in 1163. The main structure of Notre-Dame took 167 years to complete; in its transition from Romanesque to Gothic it has been described as a perfect expression of medieval architecture with its majestic towers, spire and flying buttresses.

Despite its huge size, the cathedral achieves a remarkable balance in its proportions and harmony in its facade. The superb central **rose window**, encircling a statue of the Madonna and Child, depicts the Redemption after the Fall. Look out for the **Galerie des Rois** across the top of the three doorways. The 28 statues representing the kings of

Judah and Israel have been remodelled after the drawings of the great restorer and architect Eugène Viollet-le-Duc; the original ones were pulled down during the Revolution, since they were thought to represent the kings of France. The 21 original heads discovered in 1977 are now displayed in the Musée National du Moyen Age (see page 68). Inside, the marvellous light is due in part to two more outsized rose windows, which dominate the transept. To the right of the entrance to the choir there is a lovely **statue** of the Virgin and Child.

The renowned architect, Pierre de Montreuil, is credited with much of the 13th-century construction. During the 18th century, more damage was done by the 'improvements' of redecorators of the *Ancien Régime* than by Revolutionary iconoclasts. Viollet-le-Duc carried out extensive renovations from 1845 to 1863 in response to the public outcry started by Victor Hugo's novel, *Notre-Dame de Paris*.

The only original bell remaining is the South Tower's *bourdon,* the much-admired purity of tone of which was achieved by melting down its bronze and mixing it with gold and silver donated by Louis XIV's aristocracy. If you have the energy to climb the 387 steps to the top of the south tower, you'll be rewarded with a stunning view of the city. In 2013 the cathedral celebrated its 850th anniversary, with special events and the completion of the restoration of the great organ.

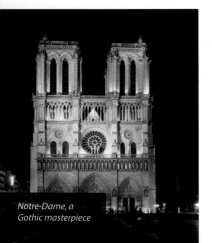
Notre-Dame, a Gothic masterpiece

Ile St-Louis

The Ile St-Louis is an enchanting little island, long popular with the more affluent gentry

Buskers on Pont St-Louis

and celebrities of Paris. More recently, President Georges Pompidou resided here (on quai de Béthune), much preferring it to the Elysée Palace. In the 17th-century **Hôtel Lambert**, on the corner of rue St-Louis-en-l'Ile, Voltaire carried on a tempestuous affair with the lady of the house, the Marquise du Châtelet.

The island's fine church, **St-Louis-en-l'Ile**, designed by Louis Le Vau, is as elegant as the mansions – bright and airy with a golden light illuminating an attractive collection of Dutch, Flemish and Italian 16th- and 17th-century art.

One of the most notable mansions is the **Hôtel Lauzun** (17 quai d'Anjou), built in the 1650s by the great architect of Versailles, Louis le Vau. Also among the island's attractions are the quiet poplar-shaded streets to the western end of quai d'Orléans with a wonderful view of the apse of Notre-Dame.

THE RIGHT BANK

The sprawling Right Bank (rive droite) covers the most luxurious shopping areas, the presidential Elysée Palace, the grands boulevards and financial

Place de la Concorde

district and, further north, seamy Clichy and Pigalle, as well as hilly Montmartre. Back in the middle of it all, the huge Louvre makes its own magnificent statement. Just to the east, Les Halles, Beaubourg (the area around the Centre Georges-Pompidou) and place de la Bastille have each been transformed by so-called Grands Projets. The lovely Marais and its Jewish quarter, representing the old Paris of the 17th century, have taken on a new fashionable appearance with the influx of trendy boutiques.

Etoile to place de la Concorde

Start at **place de l'Etoile** (officially entitled place Charles-de-Gaulle, but nobody calls it that), preferably at the top of Napoleon's monolithic **Arc de Triomphe** ⊕ (www.paris-arc-de-triomphe.fr; daily Apr–Sept 10am–11pm, Oct–Mar 10am–10.30pm) from where you'll get an excellent view of the 12-pointed star formed by the avenues radiating from the arch in Baron Haussmann's *tour de force* of geometric planning.

The Arc de Triomphe – 50m (164ft) high and 45m (148ft) wide – has become a symbol of the French nation. Napoleon himself saw only a life-sized wood-and-canvas model of the arch. King Louis-Philippe inaugurated the final version in 1836, complete with bas-reliefs and statuary celebrating the victories of the Revolution and the Napoleonic Empire.

Victor Hugo was given a magnificent funeral ceremony at the Arc de Triomphe in 1885. The Unknown Soldier of World War I was buried here in 1920, and three years later the Eternal Flame was kindled, and is still lit at 6.30pm every evening. When Hitler came to Paris as conqueror in

1940, it was the first place he wanted to see. General de Gaulle had his revenge by starting his victory parade here in 1944.

The avenues that exit from place de l'Etoile house some of the ritziest streets in Paris (avenue Foch is particularly upmarket). The **Champs-Elysées**  stretches in a straight line from the Arc de Triomphe to place de la Concorde, bordered by chestnut trees along its entirety. The first two-thirds are lined with car salesrooms, cinemas, shops and (expensive) café terraces.

After the Rond-Point, there's a pleasant, shady park that stretches down to the gigantic **place de la Concorde** ⬤. Despite its name, the square has had a tumultuous history – home to a busy guillotine in the Revolution (see page 25) and the site of the Germans' last foothold in Paris in 1944 – and handles some aggressive traffic today. In the centre is the most ancient monument in Paris, the 23m- (75ft-) tall pink granite Obelisk of Luxor from the temple of Ramses II, dating to 1300BC. It was erected here in 1836, a gift from Mohammed Ali, the viceroy of Egypt.

The Arc de Triomphe was commissioned by Napoleon as a tribute to his armies

The Louvre and its pyramid

At the eastern end of place de la Concorde is the **Jardin des Tuileries**. The gardens, characterised by geometric lawns and neat flowerbeds, are dotted with classical statuary and modern and contemporary artworks by sculptors including Rodin, Giacometti, Dubuffet, Henry Moore and Roy Lichtenstein, and are popular with Parisians out for a stroll. For children, there are marionette shows, donkey rides and sailing boats to admire on the circular ponds. In the summer months there is also a ferris wheel. Within the gardens are fragments of the royal palace (Palais des Tuileries) that once dominated the space but was destroyed by fire during the workers' uprising in 1871. Nearby, in the northwest corner of the gardens, is the **Jeu de Paume** (www.jeudepaume.org; Tue 11am–9pm, Wed–Sun 11am–7pm), an art gallery with changing exhibitions. Also in the Tuileries is the **Orangerie** (www.musee-orangerie.fr; Wed–Mon 9am–6pm), a compact museum best known for its ground-floor rooms showcasing Monet's *Nymphéas*. Downstairs is the Walter Guillaume Collection of early 20th-century works by Cézanne, Renoir, Utrillo, Henri Rousseau and Picasso.

At the eastern end of the Tuileries is the cream-coloured **Arc de Triomphe du Carrousel**, which was roughly contemporary with the larger arch at the Etoile, and is visible in a straight line beyond the Obelisk from the west. This imposing vista was originally planned for Napoleon to see from his bedroom in the Louvre.

The Louvre

Eight centuries in the making, but with nonetheless awe-inspiring architectural harmony is the **Musée du Louvre** ❻ (www.louvre.fr; Wed–Mon 9am–6pm, Fri until 9.45pm). The main entrance is through the inverted glass pyramid designed as one of Mitterrand's *grands projets* by American architect I.M. Pei. An escalator takes you down to a reception area with the ticket office, underground bookshops and cafés. Pick up a copy of the invaluable free leaflet with colour-coded floor plans at the information counter.

François I, the Louvre's first major art collector, acquired four Raphaels, three Leonardo da Vincis and one Titian (a portrait of the king himself). By 1793, when the leaders of the Revolution declared the palace a national museum, there were 650 works of art in the collection; there are now, it is estimated, some 460,000 objects of which around 35,000 are on display. If you're planning several visits, you may like to concentrate on one section at a time – the Italian, the French, the Spanish, the Flemish and Dutch, for example, but not forgetting the important sections devoted to ancient Egyptian, Greek and Roman antiquities. Artists and their works represented are outstanding and include: Michelangelo (*Two Slaves*), Leonardo (*Mona Lisa), Titian (Woman at Her Toilet),* Poussin (*Arcadian Shepherds*), Watteau (*Gilles*), Delacroix (*Liberty Leading the People*), Rubens

The Cour Carrée

Located at the eastern end of the Louvre is the Cour Carrée, which covers the original fortress built by Philippe Auguste in 1190 to protect Paris from river attack while he was away on a crusade. You can take a look at the base of the medieval towers in an excavated area.

(*Helena Fourment*), Rembrandt (*Self Portrait with a Toque*), Van Dyck (*Charles I*), Holbein (*Erasmus*), Valazquez (*Queen Marianna of Austria*), Turner (*Landscape with River and Bay*), Gainsborough (*Conversation in a Park*) among a host of works of unparalleled importance. Highlights from the **Egyptian** section include the lion-headed goddess *Sekhmet* (1400 BC) and the colossal *Amenophis IV* (1370 BC). Highlights of the **Greek** rooms include the winged *Victory of Samothrace* and the beautifully proportioned *Venus de Milo*.

In September 2012 the Department of Islamic Art opened to the public, the single largest development project since the Pyramid of 1989. The creation of French architect Rudy Ricciotti and Italian design icon Mario Bellini, it has transformed the Cour Visconti within the Louvre. Without detracting from the historical facades, the courtyard has been covered with a superb undulating glass roof creating 2,800sq metres (300,000sq ft) of exhibition space. On show are some 3,000 works spanning 1,300 years from the 8th to 19th centuries, which reflect the art of countries as diverse as Spain and India. Though physically part of the Louvre, the **Musée des Arts Décoratifs** (www.lesartsdecoratifs.fr; Tue–Sun 11am–6pm, Thu until 9pm) is a separate museum, with its own entrance at 107 rue de Rivoli. The rich permanent collection includes tapestries, furniture and porcelain, but look out for the fascinating temporary exhibitions that are held here, featuring great styles and eras of design history such as Jugendstil, Bauhaus and the American 1950s. One of the most interesting sections of the

Jardin du Palais Royal

Musée des Arts Décoratifs is devoted to fashion, textiles, and haute couture; another important area focuses on advertising and graphic design.

Palais Royal

Cross rue de Rivoli to the **Palais Royal**, built for Cardinal Richelieu as his Paris residence in 1639 and originally named Palais Cardinal. This arcaded palace, with its garden of lime trees and beeches and a pond where the young Louis XIV nearly drowned has a colourful history. In the days of Philippe d'Orléans, Regent of France during Louis XV's minority, it was the scene of notorious orgies. To pay off the extravagant family's debts, the ground-floor rooms were turned into boutiques and cafés, attracting fashionable society, together with some shady hangers-on and intellectuals. On 13 July 1789, a young firebrand, Camille Desmoulins, stood on a table at the Palais Royal's Café de Foy to deliver the speech that set off the French Revolution. The royal apartments were set ablaze in the uprising of 1871 and were subsequently restored to become the home of the Council of State and more recently of the Ministry of Culture.

Today the Palais-Royal is a chic neighbourhood of expensive apartments, shops and restaurants. Exhibitions of contemporary sculpture are held in the summer in the gardens, which also feature permanent exhibits of modern art, including Daniel Buren's zebra-striped stone columns.

Les Halles

East of the Palais Royal, the old food markets of Les Halles (now moved to less colourful surroundings in the suburb of Rungis) have been replaced by gardens, modern apartment buildings and, for the most part, the **Forum des Halles**. Once an architecturally dull, rather uninspiring shopping centre, the Forum des Halles has undergone an impressive five-year renovation, and now features a huge glass canopy that covers re-landscaped squares and gardens. The project was officially reopened by the Paris mayor, Anne Hidalgo, in April 2016 in the hope that the area will become the new heart of Paris. Around the centre, there is a lively neighbourhood of cafés, boutiques and art galleries linking up with the

Centre Pompidou that is popular with the young crowd. However, the liveliest meeting-place is around the handsome Renaissance **Fontaine des Innocents**, once part of a cemetery.

North of Les Halles is a monument with a Renaissance interior and a Gothic exterior: the church of **St-Eustache**, which is remarkable for its stained-glass windows over the choir.

Centre Pompidou

East of Les Halles is one of Europe's most important cultural centres, the **Centre National d'Art et de Culture Georges Pompidou ⓖ** (www.centre pompidou.fr; Wed–Mon 11am–9pm, Thu until 11pm), named after the French president who instigated the project. The complex is sometimes known simply as Beaubourg, after the neighbourhood that surrounds it.

A dazzling combination of public library, modern art museum, *cinémathèque,* children's workshop, industrial design centre, experimental music laboratory and outdoor entertainment area, the Centre Pompidou has become a popular destination, despite the initial upset over its unorthodox 'inside-out' design. Italian architects Renzo Piano and Gianfranco Franchi and Englishman Richard Rogers deliberately left the building's service systems visible and colour-coded: red for transportation, green for the water pipes, blue for the air-conditioning and yellow to indicate the electrical system.

A major redesign in 2000 added space to the Museum of Modern Art, which is divided into two galleries on two floors. On Level 5, the historical section (1905 to 1960) displays works by such key figures as Brancusi, Dada, Duchamp, Modigliani, Matisse, Miró and Man Ray. Presented in the contemporary collection (1960 to the present),

Defender of time

In the quartier de l'Horloge north of the Centre Pompidou is the huge Défenseur du Temps clock. On the hour, a life-size soldier does battle with either the dragon of the earth, the bird of the air or the crab of the sea. At noon and 6pm they attack simultaneously.

on Level 4, are Braque's *Man with Guitar* (1914), Matisse's collage *The Sorrow of the King* (1952), Dalí's *Six Images de Lénine sur un Piano* (1931) and Andy Warhol's *Ten Lizes* (1963).

One of the simplest pleasures here is the stunning view of Paris rooftops as you go up the escalator. And the cosmopolitan crowd outside mingling with street performers, artists and fire eaters provides hours of free entertainment.

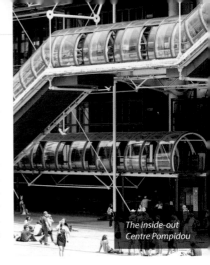
The inside-out Centre Pompidou

The Marais

North of the two islands in the river, the Marais (literally, 'swamp') district was built on land reclaimed from the marshes. It became fashionable in the 17th century, and wealthy Parisians built luxurious private homes *(hôtels particuliers)* here. Many of these Renaissance houses now serve as museums and libraries.

Take the métro to Rambuteau and start at the corner of rue des Archives and **rue des Francs-Bourgeois**, named after the poor people who were allowed to live here tax-free during the 14th century. France's National Archives are kept here in an 18th-century mansion, the **Hôtel de Soubise** (www.archives-nationales.culture.gouv.fr; Mon and Wed–Fri 10am–5.30pm, Sat–Sun 2–5.30pm), fronted by a vast horseshoe-shaped courtyard. The interior was decorated by important artists and craftsmen of the time and the apartments of the Prince and Princess of Soubise are worth seeing. Upstairs is the **Musée de l'Histoire de France** (opening hours as Hôtel de Soubise), which displays a number of important documents, including Louis XVI's diary, with its famous – and extraordinary – entry, *'Rien'* ('Nothing'), for 14 July 1789.

Eating on Place des Vosges

A garden (not always open to the public) connects the Hôtel de Soubise with its twin, the **Hôtel de Rohan**, on rue Vieille-duTemple. Look out for Robert le Lorrain's fine sculpted horses of Apollo over the old stables in the second courtyard. Two other noteworthy mansions on rue des Francs-Bourgeois are the **Hôtel Lamoignon**, at the corner of rue Pavée, and the **Hôtel Carnavalet**, once home to the illustrious 17th-century lady of letters, Madame de Sévigné, and today the Musée Historique de la Ville de Paris or **Musée Carnavalet** (www.carnavalet.paris.fr; Tue–Sun 10am-6pm).

At the end of rue des Francs-Bourgeois is what many consider to be the city's most handsome residential square, the **place des Vosges**, with its stone-and-red-brick facades. The gardens were once a favourite spot for aristocratic duels. Victor Hugo lived at No. 6, now the **Maison de Victor Hugo** (www.maisonsvictorhugo.paris.fr; Tue–Sun 10am–6pm; free), a museum of the writer's manuscripts, artefacts and drawings. Under the elegant arcades of the square are chic restaurants, boutiques and galleries.

At 5 rue de Thorigny is another of the area's major museums, the **Musée Picasso** (www.musee-picasso.fr; Tue–Sun 10am–6pm), home to over 200 paintings, 158 sculptures and hundreds of drawings, engravings, ceramics and models for theatre by the Catalan artist, and to his personal collection of masterworks by fellow artists Braque, Matisse, Miró, Degas, Renoir and Rousseau. Housed in the Hôtel Salé, a beautifully restored 17th-century mansion, the museum offers a moving portrait of the man, his family, his mistresses and friends, through letters, photograph albums, notebooks, bullfight tickets and some holiday postcards. In late 2014, the museum reopened after a major renovation: the first floor now features thematic and chronological presentations of Picasso's work; the second floor houses temporary exhibitions and a library; whilst the third floor is occupied by the archives.

Finish your visit to the Marais with a walk through the old **Jewish quarter** around the rue des Rosiers. There's a whole strip here of Jewish grocers and restaurants, selling falafels, poppy-seed cakes, apple strudels and more. Try Sacha Finkelsztajn (www.laboutiquejaune.fr), at No.27.

The Bastille

The eastern, poorer side of Paris has long been associated with the workers and social rebellion, beginning with that most famous revolutionary act of them all, the storming of the Bastille. This was the heartland of the Paris Commune, and trade unions still begin their Labour Day marches at Bastille. The old stronghold after which the large, circular place de la Bastille is named was long-since dismantled, and a bank now occupies its site. The column in the centre commemorates lives lost in the revolutions of 1830 and 1848.

For many years a run-down area, Bastille was given a boost by the construction of one of President Mitterrand's *grands projets*, the **Opéra-Bastille**. Completed in 1989, the opera house aimed to bring the traditionally élitist arts to the masses. Although critics attacked Carlos Ott's building as an unimaginative misfit, the acoustics were rated a success, and the new home of the National Opera is now an accepted part of Parisian cultural life. In the adjacent streets of this up-and-coming area, such as rue de la Couronne, traditional shops alternate with new art galleries, artists' studios, boutiques and restaurants, indicating that Mitterrand's scheme has had an effect.

Place Vendôme

The octagonal **place Vendôme** still exudes the opulence of its original conception under Louis XIV; at that time only his financiers could afford the exorbitant rents. Three centuries later, not much has changed – a score of

Opéra Garnier

international banks have their offices here, along with celebrated jewellers, the Ministry of Justice and the Ritz. The spiral of bronze bas-reliefs on the Vendôme column, commemorating Napoleon's victories and topped by a statue of the emperor, was cast from 1,250 cannons captured at Austerlitz.

The Opéra and Grands Boulevards

Wander past the goldsmiths and luxury stores of the rue de la Paix to the **Opéra Garnier** ⒣, an imposing, heavily gilded neo-Baroque building designed by Charles Garnier, a then-unknown architect who wanted to create a new 'Napoleon III' style of architecture. Completed in 1875, it is claimed to be the world's largest theatre, although the size of the stage – which can hold 450 performers – leaves room for only 2,200 spectators in the auditorium.

The boulevard des Capucines and boulevard des Italiens, known as the **Grands Boulevards**, meet at place de l'Opéra, which was a focal point in Baron Haussmann's urbanisation plans in the mid-19th century. Today you will find elegant boutiques around the square, as well as the famous Café de la Paix, and the boulevards are where you will find some of the most popular cinemas. Behind the Opéra are two of France's best-known department stores *(grands magasins)*, the Galeries Lafayette and Au Printemps.

Westwards along boulevard Haussmann, at No. 158, is the lovely **Musée Jacquemart-André ❶** (daily 10am–6pm; www.musee-jacquemart-andre.com), in the elegant residence of a famous 19th-century collector, Edouard André, and showcasing one of France's finest gatherings of 18th-century French, 17th-century Flemish and Dutch and Italian Renaissance art, in much the same vein as New York's Frick Collection or London's Wallace Collection. It also houses a beautiful tearoom. As boulevard Haussmann runs east, it turns into boulevard Montmartre. At No. 10 is the **Musée Grévin** (www.grevin-paris.com; Mon–Fri 10am–6pm, Sat–Sun 9.30am–7pm), an excellent waxworks museum, with special exhibitions for children.

Place de la Madeleine

Dominating the north side of **Place de la Madeleine ❶** is the Greco-Roman Ste-Marie Madeleine (www.eglise-lamadeleine.com; daily 9.30am–7pm; free), commonly referred to as the **Madeleine**. Originally planned under Louis XV and begun in 1764 it wasn't consecrated until 1842. During that period, competing plans called for it to be a bank, a railway station and a memorial to Napoleon and his armies. It's popular for the flower market at its base and the grand **view** afforded from the top of the steps down rue Royale to the place de la Concorde.

Down on the right is Maxim's restaurant, which began as an ice-cream parlour and is now almost as much of a Parisian institution as the Madeleine. Cutting across rue Royale, **rue du Faubourg-Saint-Honoré** is the city's most luxurious shopping street. At No. 55 are the heavily guarded gates of the French president's Elysée Palace.

Place d'Iéna and Palais de Chaillot

Further east on the banks of the Seine is the **Musée d'Art Moderne de Paris** (www.mam.paris.fr; Tue–Sun 10am–6pm, Thu until 9.30pm for special exhibitions), which has an important collection of 20th-century art displayed in the spacious galleries of the Palais de Tokyo. Close by, on place d'Iéna, is the **Musée Guimet** (www.guimet.fr; Wed–Mon 10am–6pm), which has a superb collection of Indian, Japanese and Chinese art. Facing the Eiffel Tower across the banks of the Seine lie the **Jardins du Trocadéro** and the **Palais de Chaillot**. This 1930s' building houses the Théâtre National de Chaillot, as well as – in the west wing – the **Musée National de la Marine** (Museum of Naval History; www.musee-marine.fr; closed for renovation) and the **Musée de l'Homme** (Museum of Anthropology; www.museedelhomme.fr; Wed–Mon 11am–7pm). The east wing houses the **Cité de l'Architecture**, a museum of France's architectural history (www.citechaillot.fr; Wed–Mon 11am–7pm, Thu until 9pm).

Montmartre and Pigalle

Long famous as the home of artists and bohemians, who refer to it as 'La Butte' ('The Mound') and a lively nightspot, being home to such fabled haunts as the club Au Lapin Agile, **Montmartre Ⓚ** is an essential piece of the Paris mythology. This mystique is not confined to the 19th century – the area was the setting for the highly romanticised view of Parisian life in the film *Amélie*. According to legend, the hill was originally named Mons Martyrum – where, after being decapitated, St Denis, the first bishop of Paris, picked up his head and walked away. However, scholars claim that it was really named Mons Mercurii and was the site of a pagan Roman temple.

In appearance, Montmartre bears close resemblance to the little country village of 400 years ago, with narrow, winding, hilly streets and dead ends. It's best to leave the car behind and take the Porte de la Chapelle *métro* line from Concorde to Abbesses. (You can also take the funicular railway up from rue Tardieu.)

From the place des Abbesses, take rue Ravignan to 13 place Emile-Goudeau. This was the site of the **Bateau-Lavoir** studio, an unprepossessing glass-roofed loft reconstructed following a 1970 fire. Here Picasso, Braque and Juan Gris developed Cubism, while Modigliani painted, and Apollinaire wrote his first surrealistic verses. Nearby, their illustrious predecessors Renoir, Van Gogh and Gauguin lived and worked in the rues Cortot, de l'Abreuvoir and St-Rustique (site of the restaurant A la Bonne Franquette, where Van Gogh painted *La Guinguette*).

Painters and tourists alike still throng the **place du Tertre**, Montmartre's historic 'village' square, where marriages were announced and criminals hanged. The whole area retains a village feel, with a slow pace of life, a variety of street performers and pleasant cafés. On rue St-Vincent, at the corner of rue des Saules, look out for Paris's own vineyard, the Clos de Montmartre.

At the other end of rue St-Vincent, you will come around the back of the 19th-century Romano-Byzantine basilica **Sacré-Cœur** (www.sacre-coeurmontmartre.com; daily 6.30am–10.30pm; free entry, charge for dome), towering over Paris with its gleaming white facade and distinctive domes and arches. Inside are splendid mosaics, but most visitors are transfixed by the views over the descending steps and gardens to the landmarks of the city below.

Below Montmartre is the **Pigalle** district, home to street prostitutes, strip clubs, sex shops, hip bars and cabarets – and the Moulin Rouge. Although the area has an element of hip dance venues and bars for Paris's young crowd, it is still quite seedy and you will need to be wary, especially at night.

La Villette

In the northeast corner of the city (*métro* Porte de la Villette), this area has been converted

An original Art Nouveau Métro entrance at Abbesses

from what was the world's biggest slaughterhouse into a futuristic complex of cultural and scientific activities. La Villette's **Cité des Sciences et de l'Industrie** (www.cite-sciences.fr; Tue–Sat 10am–6pm, Sun 10am–7pm) puts the accent on public participation. The **Explora** science museum has exciting exhibits on everything from astronomy and mathematics to computer science. There is also a planetarium, a **Cité des Enfants** for those under 12 years, and the shining stainless steel **Géode** sphere, which contains a revolutionary cinema with a hemispheric screen 36m (118ft) in diameter. Opposite is the **Philharmonie de Paris** (www.philharmoniedeparis.fr), Paris' major music complex, boasting the **Grand Hall**, designed by Jean Nouvel and opened in 2015, along with the **Cité de la Musique**, which houses the **Musée de la Musique**. Nearby is the **Zénith** concert hall.

THE LEFT BANK

The fashion and media worlds are gradually supplanting the intellectuals in their time-honoured stronghold on the Left Bank (rive gauche). Writers and painters who used to congregate in the cafés of Saint-Germain-des-Prés seem to have been squeezed out by film directors, TV celebrities, advertising people – and more and more tourists. There is much more to the Left Bank than the student life of the Latin Quarter,

PÈRE LACHAISE

The grounds of the cemeteries of Paris are beautifully kept, and the avenues of stone tombs provide a fascinating walk through history. In the largest, the **Cimetière du Père-Lachaise** (mid-Mar–Oct Mon–Fri 8am–6pm, Sat 8.30am–6pm, Sun 9am–6pm, Nov–mid-Mar until 5.30pm; free), 1,350,000 people have been buried since its foundation in 1804. A map available at the entrance will help you to locate the tombs of the famous, including Rossini, La Fontaine, Chopin, Molière, Sarah Bernhardt, Oscar Wilde and Jim Morrison.

but so many schools and colleges are packed into a small area that it's the young who set the pace.

Montparnasse took over from Montmartre as the haunt of the avant-garde in the 1920s, and the area still stakes a claim. The Left Bank has its share of monuments and museums, and the Luxembourg gardens remain an evergreen favourite.

The Latin Quarter

The origin of the name comes from the 13th century, when the city's first university moved from the cloisters of Notre-Dame to the Left Bank and the young came to the *quartier* to learn Latin. In those days *l'université* meant merely a collection of people – students who met on a street corner, or in a public square or courtyard, to hear a teacher lecture from a bench or from an upstairs window or balcony. These days the students attend overcrowded classrooms, but the tradition of lively open-air discussion continues, often over an endlessly nursed coffee or glass of wine in one of the pavement cafés on boulevard St-Michel or in the streets around the faculty buildings.

The narrow streets near the exquisite 13th-century Flamboyant Gothic church of St-Séverin – rues de la Huchette, de la Harpe and St-Séverin – evoke a medieval world infused with the cuisines of many countries and tiny independent cinemas.

Close to the crossroads of the area's two great thoroughfares, boulevard Saint-Germain and boulevard St-Michel, is the **Musée National du Moyen Age** Ⓛ (6 place Paul-Painlevé; www.musee-moyenage.fr; Tue–Sun 9.30am–6.15pm), a sumptuous collection of medieval tapestries, sculpture and precious artefacts displayed in the authentic setting of one the city's finest Gothic mansions, alongside traces of Roman Paris

Nearby, on busy **place St-Michel**, students buy textbooks and stationery and linger around the ornate Second Empire fountain. Directly behind the square sits the main building of the **Sorbonne**. Founded in 1253 as a college for poor theological students by Robert de Sorbon, Louis IX's chaplain, it took shape as a university under the tutelage of Cardinal Richelieu. Students protesting against overcrowding, antiquated methods of

The beautifully landscaped
Jardin du Luxembourg

teaching and stifling bureaucracy made the Sorbonne a focal point in 1968. When the police invaded its precincts – which for centuries had guaranteed student immunity – the rebellion erupted into the streets. The Sorbonne has since been integrated into the larger Paris university system and lost its independence.

Around the corner is the huge, domed neoclassical **Panthéon** (www.paris-pantheon.fr; daily Apr–Sep 10am–6.30pm, Oct–Mar 10am–6pm). It was originally intended as a church for Louis XV, but is now a secular mausoleum of some of the nation's greatest heroes. In the crypt are interred the remains of Voltaire, Jean-Jacques Rousseau, Victor Hugo and Emile Zola, assassinated Socialist leader Jean Jaurès and Louis Braille. More recent heroes buried here include the World War II Resistance fighter Jean Moulin and the scientist Marie Curie, the only woman to be honoured in such a way.

Further up boulevard St-Michel, away from the river, is the large **Jardin du Luxembourg Ⓜ**. Despite their 17th-century origins, these gardens avoid the rigid geometry of the Tuileries and the gardens at Versailles. The horse chestnuts, beeches and plane trees, the orangery and ornamental pond inspired the bucolic paintings of Jean-Antoine Watteau.

Back down by the Seine, but to the east, is one of the most striking buildings on the riverbank, the **Institut du Monde Arabe** (Arab World Institute; www.imarabe.org; Tue–Fri 10am–6pm, Sat–Sun 10am–7pm), which was designed by architect Jean Nouvel in 1987. Its fine Arabesque lattice-work windows have thousands of photosensitive apertures, which regulate the light entering the building. Fine views are to be had from the rooftop café.

Existential cafés

Situated close to the church of Saint-Germain-des-Prés are two Parisian literary institutions, the Café de Flore and Les Deux Magots. These archetypal Parisian cafés are famous as the meeting places for the 1950s' and 1960s' existentialists. Budding philosophers can join discussion groups at the Café de Flore in English first Wednesday of the month from 7 to 9pm and online via Zoom every other week.

Saint-Germain-des-Prés

Saint-Germain-des-Prés is the literary quarter of Paris – home of publishing houses, bookish cafés, the Académie Française and chic boutiques competing with bookshops, art galleries and antiques shops. The cafés around **place Saint-Germain-des-Prés** act as the 'village centre'. On the north side is the Café Bonaparte, and on the west Les Deux Magots, famous for its associations with 1950s' existentialists Jean-Paul Sartre and Simone de Beauvoir. Further up the boulevard is the Café de Flore, which has also tapped into the public fascination with the neighbourhood's intellectual history. Although now somewhat overpriced, they do both provide what still feels like the ultimate Parisian café experience.

Nearby, the **church** of Saint-Germain-des-Prés is an attractive mixture of Romanesque and Gothic styles, with an 11th-century clock tower. To the north of the church, the rue Bonaparte takes you to the prestigious **Ecole des Beaux-Arts** (www.beauxartsparis.fr), the country's foremost school of art. Incorporated in its structure are fragments of medieval and Renaissance architecture and sculpture.

Musée d'Orsay

Tucked away at No. 5 place de Furstenberg is the **Musée National Eugène Delacroix** (www.musee-delacroix.fr; Wed–Mon 9.30am–5.30pm). Compared with the artist's paintings at the Louvre and the Musée d'Orsay, as well as his frescoes in the church of St-Sulpice, the work on show in his former flat is intimate, including sketches and pastel studies as well as work relating to his friendship with the poet Baudelaire.

Rue de Seine, which is renowned for its art galleries, leads north of here to the river. On quai Conti, by the Pont des Arts, is the **Institut de France**, the handsome home of the august Académie Française. It was built by Louis Le Vau in 1668 to harmonise with the Louvre across the river and the academy was founded by Cardinal Richelieu as the supreme arbiter of the French language. The academy's lifetime members, known as *'Les Immortels'*, produce edicts on French terminology and usage; among words recently – and controversially – legalised were *le ketchup* and *le hamburger*.

Musée d'Orsay

Northwest along the river is France's national museum of 19th-century art, housed within spectacular premises. The 19th-century Orsay railway station was transformed in 1980 into the **Musée d'Orsay** **N** (www.musee-orsay.fr; Tue–Sun 9.30am–6pm, Thu until 9.45pm), which embraces the nation's extensive creativity from 1848 to 1914 in painting, sculpture, architecture and industrial design, advertising, newspapers, book publishing, photography and the early years of cinema. A new gallery to house the stunning Impressionist works using superb artificial lighting and costing some €10 million was opened in late 2011, completing part of a €25 million two-year renovation programme.

Around the Invalides

The **Hôtel des Invalides** **O** was built by Louis XIV as France's first national hospital for soldiers. Today it houses a number of museums, the most important of which is the **Musée de l'Armée** (www.musee-armee.fr; daily 10am–6pm, Thurs until 9pm) with exhibits stretching as far back as the Stone Age. Set in the crypt directly beneath the Invalides' golden dome, **Napoleon's tomb** is awesomely elaborate. His body, dressed in the green uniform of the Chasseurs de la Garde, is encased in six coffins, one inside the other. The innermost coffin is of iron, the next of mahogany, then two of lead, one of ebony and the outer one of oak. The monument of red porphyry from Finland rests on a pedestal of green granite, encircled by pillars sculpted by Pradier. Also in the crypt are the remains of Napoleon's son, brought to France from Vienna by Hitler in 1940. The military complex continues with the Ecole Militaire and the spacious gardens of the **Champ-de-Mars**, once used for military exercises and the series of World's Fairs held between 1867 and 1937.

The fascinating **Musée Rodin** ⓟ (www.musee-rodin.fr; Tue–Sun 10am–6.30pm), with its attractive sculpture garden and children's play area, is on the rue de Varenne next to the Hôtel des Invalides. Works displayed include *The Kiss* and *The Thinker*, along with macquettes showing how compositions including *The Burghers of Calais* were created.

The Eiffel Tower

There are monuments that you can ignore and those you have to look at twice, and then there is the **Tour Eiffel** ⓠ (www.tour-eiffel.fr; daily 9.30am–10.45pm for lifts and steps, winter until 6pm for steps, check website for seasonal changes). Monuments usually celebrate heroes, commemorate victories or honour kings or saints, but the Eiffel Tower is a monument for its own sake. Its construction for the World's Fair of 1889 was an astounding engineering achievement – some 18,000 pieces joined together by 2.5 million rivets, soaring 300m (984ft) into the air, but standing on a base that is only 130m (1,400ft) square.

Long live the Emperor

Napoleon's grandiose 1804 coronation in Notre-Dame was attended by Pope Pious VII. The latter stopped short at crowning the diminutive emperor's head, but with the Pope's blessing, Napoleon simply crowned himself while the crowd cried 'Vive l'Empereur!'

The tower was slated for destruction in 1910, but no-one had the heart to go through with it, despite the behemoth's vociferous critics. Writer Guy de Maupassant signed a manifesto against 'this vertiginously ridiculous tower', and the poet Verlaine rerouted his journey around Paris to avoid seeing it. Nowadays, everybody seems to love it. It has a chic brasserie on the first platform, a gourmet restaurant on the second, a champagne bar on the third and a view from the top stretching as far as the eye can see on a clear day.

Just before the Eiffel Tower on the Left Bank is the **Musée du Quai Branly** (www.quaibranly.fr; Tue–Sun 10.30am–7pm, Thu until 10pm). The collection is devoted to the arts of Africa, Asia, Oceania and America, and includes objects as diverse as a Hawaiian chief's helmet and a Siberian shaman's cloak.

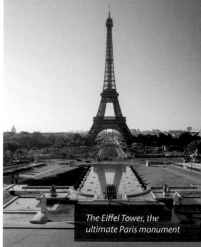
The Eiffel Tower, the ultimate Paris monument

Montparnasse

In the 1920s, Montparnasse took over from Montmartre as the stomping ground of the capital's artistic colony, or at least that of its avant-garde. American expatriates such as Ernest Hemingway, F. Scott Fitzgerald, Gertrude Stein, John Dos Passos, and Theodore Dreiser contributed to the free-living mystique.

While other quarters are known for their fine palaces and churches, Montparnasse, named after a 17th-century gravel mound since removed, has cafés and bars for its landmarks, the majority of them along **boulevard du Montparnasse**: the Closerie des Lilas; the Select, a Henry Miller hang-out; La Coupole, a favourite brasserie of Jean-Paul Sartre and Simone de Beauvoir; the Dôme and the Rotonde.

Towering over the *quartier* and considered by many to be an eyesore is the 59-floor **Tour Montparnasse** office block (www.tourmontparnasse 56.com; Apr–Sept daily 9.30am–11.30pm, Oct–Mar Sun–Thu 9.30am–10.30pm, Fri–Sat until 11pm) – there are excellent views from the top.

The Grande Arche at La Défense

WEST PARIS

Among Baron Haussmann's additions to the city is the **Bois de Boulogne**, 900 hectares (2,224 acres) of parkland on the western edge of the city, with lakes, restaurants, cafés and meadows filled with picnicking Parisians in the summer months. One of the main attractions is the **Parc de Bagatelle**, a walled garden with the city's most beautiful display of flowers. For children, the **Jardin d'Acclimatation** offers a miniature railway, a puppet theatre, pony rides, an aviary with nearly 200 birds and a collection of farm animals. It's best to avoid the park after dark, as it's notorious for its seedier side, such as prostitution and drug-dealing.

Further west is **La Défense**, Europe's largest business centre, which was given a focus in 1989 with the opening of another of Mitterrand's *grands projets*, the **Grande Arche de la Défense**. The arch forms an axis with the Louvre, place de la Concorde and the Arc de Triomphe.

ILE-DE-FRANCE

VERSAILLES

Just 21km (15 miles) from the capital, **Versailles** ❷ (www.chateau versailles.fr; Apr–Oct palace Tue–Sun 9am–6.30pm, gardens 8am–8.30pm, Nov–Mar palace 9am–5.30pm, gardens 8am–6pm) is an easy (although full) day trip. Organised bus tours start at the Tuileries on the rue de Rivoli side. However, the palace and gardens are so enormous that you may prefer to see them at your own pace, leaving out what your head and feet can't take. A little train can take you on a 35-minute tour of the gardens, with commentary in French and English; bicycles are also available for rent.

With a little advance planning, you can transform an otherwise tiring day into a delightful treat. Try the following agenda: an early start at a Paris street market to buy a picnic; a morning tour of the palace; a stroll through the palace gardens to lunch beside the Grand Canal; a siesta and tea in the gardens of the Petit Trianon; finally, a wander back across the palace gardens for a last view of the great château.

The Palace

If you don't already have a clear idea of what kind of man Louis XIV was, take a long, hard look at his palace. Never did a piece of architecture more exactly express the personality of its builder than the Château de Versailles – extravagant, pompous, dazzling, formidable, glorious and vain.

The view of Versailles from the gardens

Delicate statuary

Louis XIII had hoped to make his favourite hunting lodge a modest retirement home. But his son turned Versailles into a self-centred universe that was far from modest, proclaiming his own grandeur in a vast, sprawling edifice of stone and brick, marble, gilt and crystal. The palace has been splendidly restored since World War I with the help of private contributions, most notably from John D. Rockefeller. Where the original furnishings and decoration were missing, superb appropriate equivalents have been installed.

The self-guide tour begins at the intimate **Royal Chapel**, a harmonious mix of white marble, Corinthian columns, and Baroque murals with gilded altar and balustrades. The royal family worshipped upstairs, looking down onto the courtiers in the nave.

In the rooms of the **Grands Appartements**, named after the gods and goddesses whom Louis felt to be his appropriate companions, the king entertained his courtiers. In the **Salon de Diane**, the billiard table has gone, but Bernini has left a superb bust of the king as reigning champion at 27. The ceiling painting of the Sun King in his chariot and pictorial references to Alexander the Great and Caesar make it abundantly clear the **Salon d'Apollon** was Louis XIV's throne room.

But by far the most striking of these lavish royal apartments is the glittering **Galerie des Glaces** (Hall of Mirrors), built to catch every ray of the setting sun in the 17 tall arched panels of mirrors. This was the palace's grandest reception hall, where the king gave his wildest parties and received his most important foreign envoys. Le Brun's paintings depict Louis XIV's wars in Holland and his more peaceful achievements at home.

In the **Queen's Bedroom** 19 royal children were born, many of them – as was the custom of the time – with the public looking on.

On a separate guided tour, you can visit the **Royal Opera** of Louis XV and the king's private apartments. The **King's Bedroom**, with two portraits by Van Dyck, is set at the exact centre of the sun's path from east to west. The court was encouraged to come here every day to witness the monarch's waking and retiring. Louis XIV died here in 1715 from gangrene of the leg.

The Gardens

If English and Japanese gardens attempt, in their different ways, to enhance nature by 'tidying it up' while imitating a 'natural' landscape, the French garden, as epitomised by Versailles, aims to impose a formal pattern. Resuming a tradition of Classical Rome in his work at Versailles,

VERSAILLES: THE NUMBERS

Louis XIV's Versailles served two purposes: it provided him with a large residence and it drew his courtiers away from the cafés and conspiracies of Paris, giving him more absolute control over the state. Designed to lodge 3,000 noblemen and servants, the palace took 50 years to build, spanning the whole of his reign. Some parts were still incomplete at his death.

Louis Le Vau and Jules Hardouin-Mansart were the principal architects, while Charles Lebrun directed the interior design and monumental sculpture, and André Le Nôtre laid out the gardens. Of the 36,000-strong workforce (plus 6,000 horses), 227 men died on the job. There are 11 hectares (27 acres) of roof, 2,153 windows, 700 rooms, 67 staircases, 51,210 square metres of floor, 50 fountains, and 35km (22 miles) of water conduits.

The impossibly lavish Galerie des Glaces

André Le Nôtre used the paths and avenues of trees and statuary to divide flowerbeds, ponds and fountain basins into intricate geometric patterns. Pause for a moment at the palace's western terrace alongside the Galerie des Glaces for a first view of his asymmetrical arrangement of the grounds.

As you make your way through the gardens, look back occasionally at the changing perspectives of the palace. Directly beyond the western terrace is the *Axe du Soleil* (Path of the Sun) leading down to the **Bassin d'Apollon**. Adorned with sculptures of Greek mythology, this and the **Bassin de Neptune** and **Bassin du Dragon** in the northeast corner served as centrepieces for royal garden parties. Beyond the Bassin d'Apollon is the **Grand Canal**, on which the king kept his Venetian gondolas. Today, you can rent small rowing boats.

On Sunday afternoons from April to September, the great waters of the Apollo, Neptune and Dragon fountains are turned on, with a backdrop of Baroque music, recapturing some of the splendour of festivities at the court of the Sun King. The traditional son-et-lumière (sound-and-light) shows are still held on Saturday nights from June to September.

To the northwest of the château, the **Grand Trianon** palace, surrounded by pleasantly unpompous gardens, was the home of Louis XIV's mistress, Madame de Maintenon, where the ageing king increasingly took refuge.

The picturesque **Petit Trianon**, where Marie-Antoinette tried to hide from the Revolution, has the allure of a doll's house in comparison with the rest of Versailles. Its gardens, with ponds, mounds and shady woods, have the feel of an English country garden and make a relaxing change from the grandiose formality of the château. The childlike playfulness of the doomed queen's hideaway is reinforced by the **Hameau**, a hamlet of little thatched cottages where she and her retinue reputedly pretended to be milkmaids and farm boys.

CHARTRES

One of the most moving experiences on a journey through France is your first view of the silhouette of **Notre-Dame de Chartres Cathedral** (www.cathedrale-chartres.org; daily 8.30am–7.30pm) towering over the city of **Chartres ❸**, and the wheat fields of the fertile Beauce plain. It's a pleasant one-hour drive southwest from Paris, and there are regular train departures from the Gare de Montparnasse. This masterpiece of French civilisation marks the transition in the 12th century from the solid, sober Romanesque style of the church's beginnings to the more airy, assertive Gothic of its ascendancy.

Boating along the Grand Canal at Versailles

As you face the harmoniously asymmetrical western facade, the **Clocher Vieux** (old tower) is a prime example of Romanesque simplicity, whereas the taller **Clocher Neuf** (new tower) is lighter, with its slender, more ornate steeple.

On the central porch, the **Portail Royal**, the stately, deliberately elongated sculptures of Old Testament figures contrast with the freer, more vigorous statuary that adorns the church's northern and southern porches.

Perhaps the most famous feature of the cathedral is its 173 **stained-glass windows**. Their unique 'Chartres blue' and deep red bring an ethereal light into the nave, especially when the late-afternoon sun is shining through the western rose window, depicting the Last Judgment. On the southern side of the choir among the oldest and most famous of the windows is an enthroned Mary with Jesus on her lap, **Notre-Dame de la Belle Verrière**. The church is dedicated to Mary, representing her 175 times in the various sculptures and windows.

In the paving of the centre aisle of the nave is a large circular **labyrinth**. Medieval penitents traced its path on hands and knees, from the edge to the centre, in a symbolic spiritual journey.

Back outside, from the Episcopal Garden, at the rear of the cathedral, a stairway takes you down to the **old town**. Its streets of attractive 16th- and 17th-century houses, built along the banks of the Eure, offer pretty views of the cathedral.

FONTAINEBLEAU

The huge royal **palace** (www.chateaudefontainebleau.fr; Wed–Mon Apr–Sept 9.30am–6pm, Oct–Mar 9.30am–5pm) of

Chez Monet

Claude Monet's house (www.fondation-monet.com; Apr–Oct daily 9.30am–6pm) at Giverny is 85km (53 miles) northwest of Paris by the A13, D181 and D5 (also accessible by train from Gare St-Lazare to Vernon). Its pond, Japanese bridge and water lilies inspired some of Impressionism's most famous works.

Fontainebleau ❹ is an elegant monument to the Renaissance tastes of François I and Henri IV, although subsequent monarchs made additions and refurbished it. Key features are the horseshoe-shaped **staircase** *(Escalier du Fer-à-Cheval)* at the end of the stately front courtyard, the **Cour du Cheval Blanc**; the Renaissance ballroom and the allegorical paintings in the **Galerie François I**.

Napoleon refurnished the palace after the looting of the Revolution and abdicated here in 1814 to go into his first exile. **Napoleon's apartments** display the style of his empire, and a Napoleonic museum has been installed in the Louis XV wing.

Although there's enough to see inside Fontainebleau to keep you busy for a full day, many visitors also spend their time exploring the beautiful grounds and the spectacular **Forest of Fontainebleau** – 25,000 hectares (over 60,000 acres) of oak, beech, silver birch, pine, chestnut and hornbeam.

You can opt for a leisurely walk or a lengthy hike on well-marked paths. Climbers will find a miniature mountain range of sheer rock faces and cliffs; the most popular are the rugged **Gorges de Franchard**, west of the palace. However, many visitors find the Gorges d'Apremont (near the town of Barbizon, a haunt of 19th-century landscape painters) less crowded.

PARC ASTÉRIX AND DISNEYLAND RESORT PARIS

Families with children – even those unfamiliar with the comic-book character and his Gallic resistance to the Roman invaders – will enjoy a change of pace and a day visit to the **Parc Astérix** theme park (www.parcasterix.fr; mid Apr–Aug daily, Sept–Oct Sat–Sun 10am–7pm). Attractions include a dolphin pool, a medieval encampment, some inventive water rides, and scary roller coasters. The park is 22 miles (35km) north of Paris on the A1. Buses run to the Roissy-Charles de Gaulle transportation hub.

An alternative is **Disneyland Resort Paris ❺** (tel: 01 60 30 60 53; www.disneylandparis.com; hours vary, call ahead or check website), 32km (20 miles) east of Paris near Marne-la-Vallée. Opened in 1992 and initially vilified by the French press, the epitome of all things American

Poppies on the Somme battlefields

is now the No. 1 attraction in the heart of 'Old Europe'.

The resort receives tens of thousands of visitors every day and all the Disney standards are here: the afternoon parades of characters, bare-knuckle rides, stunt show spectaculars and fireworks displays in the evening. Disney Village has restaurants, nightclubs and a massive multiscreen cinema. TGV trains run from Roissy-Charles de Gaulle airport and buses from Orly airport.

Château de Fontainebleau

THE NORTHEAST

The northeastern section of France offers everything from high coastal dunes and rolling farmland to picturesque mountains, forests and vineyards. The picturesque villages of Flanders abound with flowers in the summer, while the region's larger towns – Lille, Arras, and Amiens to the north, Reims in the centre, and Nancy and Strasbourg to the east – exude civic pride.

Flanders, Picardy, Alsace and Lorraine bear the scars of many wars. The English were victorious in the fields of Crécy (1346) and Azincourt (Agincourt, 1415). A line of fortifications was built at Calais, Dunkerque, Douai, Valenciennes and Lille for Louis XIV's wars against the Netherlands in the 17th century. Flanders and the river valleys of the Somme and Marne were major battlefields of World War I, and are dotted with memorials and military cemeteries.

Deeper into the interior, Burgundy is famous for its vineyards. Historically it was the stronghold of the dukes of Dijon, alongside the ecclesiastical empires of the Cluny and Cistercian monasteries.

NORD-PAS-DE-CALAIS

Visitors to France often overlook the charms of the far north. If you're coming into France from the English Channel or across the Belgian border, rather than rushing south on the *autoroute*, plan a leisurely journey through the Nord-pas-de-Calais region and on the smaller roads of Picardy.

Le Touquet and Boulogne-sur-Mer

The seaside resort of **Le Touquet** was established at the end of the 19th century, when swimming became all the rage for its beneficial health effects. Today, it is more stylish than many other French coastal towns, with plenty to please both adults and children, from casinos and upmarket shops to excellent watersports facilities.

Half an hour's drive north is historic **Boulogne-sur-Mer** ❻. The town's hilly site made it a strategic point for both defenders of France and invaders of England, from the Romans to Napoleon and Hitler. It is divided into

Positive thinking at Le Touquet

two parts, the old upper town or Haute Ville and the modern lower town. Children love the excellent sea-life centre, **Nausicaä** (www.nausicaa.fr; daily 9.30am–6.30pm, shut for around two weeks in January).

Montreuil-sur-Mer

Around an hour's drive south of Calais, the medieval walled town of **Montreuil-sur-Mer** sits high above the valley of the river Canche. Montreuil was a thriving port before the river silted up in the 1300s (the sea is now 25km away). Today it is a busy market town and gastronomic destination, with far more than its fair share of quality restaurants and food producers and and reatilers.

Victor Hugo used the town as a setting for *Les Misérables,* and each summer (usually at the end of July) the residents stage a retrospective son-et-lumière performance in the **Citadelle,** parts of which date from the 9th century.

A walk around the shaded top of the ramparts takes about half an hour and offers beautiful views of the surrounding countryside. Longer hikes follow well-marked trails across the fields.

Hesdin and Les Sept Vallées

The river Canche flows right through the centre of the small town of Hesdin, disappearing under buildings and hump-backed bridges. The Flemish/Spanish **Hôtel de Ville** which dominates the market square has a magnificent porch (if you can pick your time to visit, try to arrive on Thursday morning, for the weekly market). The nearby **Eglise Notre Dame** also manages to combine Flemish architecture with a Renaissance porch.

The battlefield at **Azincourt** (Agincourt) is 15km (9 miles) north of Hesdin, just off the D928. The **Centre Historique Médiéval** (azincourt1415.com; daily 10am–5.30pm, July–Aug until 6.30pm) offers a tour of the site of Henry's victory of 1415.

Leaving Azincourt, continue north to Fruges. In Fruges take the small D130 southwest towards Créquy, following the valley of the

Cafés line the Grand' Place in Lille

tiny Créquoise river back down to the Canche. Cross the Canche and continue south to Buire-le-Sec and the village of **Maintenay**, where a restored 12th-century mill now sells homemade bread and serves lunches in a wonderfully cool and leafy setting.

Across the river Authie and a few minutes' drive east is the 18th-century **Abbaye de Valloires** (www.abbaye-valloires.com; tel: 03 22 29 62 33; daily mid-Mar–mid-Nov; hours vary considerably; guided tours only) whose huge gardens display more than 5,000 species and varieties of plants, many from China and Japan, including a large collection of old-fashioned and wild roses, presented in a number of formal and informal settings.

St-Omer

Prosperous from its involvement in the textile industry since the Middle Ages, this town survived bombardment in two world wars and remains a bustling centre with an impressive main square.

Once a cathedral, the 13th-century **Basilique Notre-Dame** can be hard to find among the narrow cobbled streets of the old town. It has a fine south porch and marble and alabaster treasures that evoke the wealth of the diocese in the 16th and 17th centuries. The chapel screens are particularly elaborate and in the northern arm of the transept there is an intricate 16th-century astronomical clock.

The museum at the **Hôtel Sandelin** (www.musees-saint-omer.fr; Wed–Sun 10am–noon, 2pm–6pm) is well worth a visit, both for the splendid 18th-century mansion with its Louis XV furnishings and for its rich collections of porcelain, including St-Omer faïence and Delftware.

Lille

At the centre of the fourth-largest urban area in France and a major high-speed train (TGV and Eurostar) hub, **Lille** ❼ has come a long way since its humble beginnings as a small island on the River Deûle. It was a major industrial centre in the 19th century and is a dynamic cultural showcase at the start of the 21st. This impressive development, coupled with the city's status as a fought-over border town, pervades its architecture, art collections, cuisine and culture, offering much to the visitor. The best place to start a tour is the heart of the old city, **Vieux Lille**. Here, there are well-preserved streets of narrow brick-and-stone Flemish houses, many recently restored and now containing upmarket shops, regional restaurants and lively bars that point to the city's recent renaissance as well as its historic one.

Place du Général de Gaulle (also known as the Grand' Place), the heart of Vieux Lille, is home to the splendid 17th-century **Vieille Bourse** (Old Exchange) and grand **Opéra**. Nearby is the **Cathédrale Notre-Dame-de-la-Treille**, a more recent curiosity.

Other highlights include the **Palais des Beaux-Arts** (place

Swimming in art

Close to Lille, Roubaix has been put on the tourist map by La Piscine (www.roubaix-lapiscine.com; 23 rue de l'Espérance; Tue–Thu 11am–6pm, Fri 11am–8pm, Sat, Sun 1–6pm), an art gallery in a stunningly converted art-deco swimming pool.

de la République; www.pba-lille.fr; Mon 2–6pm, Wed–Sun 10am–6pm), Lille's fine-arts museum, generally considered to be second only to the Louvre in France.

Lens

Though primarily an industrial city, Lens, 40km (25 miles) south of Lille, was chosen to house the outpost gallery for the **Louvre** (www.louvre lens.fr; Wed–Mon 10am–6pm). Opened in December 2012 it is part of a planned regeneration of the area, bringing fine art to a new audience and displaying works from the huge store at the Louvre in Paris.

Arras

Arras was famous in the Middle Ages for its production of cloth and hanging tapestries. The town, just off the *autoroute* from Calais, has two of the most beautiful city squares in France – the arcades and the gabled facades of the **Grand' Place** and the **place des Héros** echo the classical Flemish style of the 17th and 18th centuries. View the town and surrounding countryside from the belfry of the **Hôtel de Ville** (May–Sept Mon–Sat 9am–6.30pm, Sun 10am–1pm, 2.30–6.30pm, shorter hours in winter) or go down to the basement and take the guided tour of the *Boves*, a labyrinth of underground passages which have served as quarries, soldiers' billets and cellars and now house shops and restaurants. Arras was the birthplace of the French Revolutionary leader Maximilien Robespierre, and his former home on rue Robespierre is now a **museum** (temporarily closed; when open: May–Sept Tue–Fri 2–5.30pm, Sat–Sun 2.30–6.30pm, shorter hours in winter).

PICARDY

St-Valéry-sur-Somme and Péronne

William the Conqueror set sail for England in 1066 from this small fishing port at the mouth of the Somme. Today **St-Valéry ❽** offers ramparts and half-timbered houses in the Haute Ville, and a pleasant waterfront promenade with views of seals in the estuary. Children will enjoy the little steam train that loops around the bay to Le Crotoy in the summer. The surrounding area is well known for its bird life. A tour of the beautiful **Parc Ornithologique de Marquenterre** at St-Quentin-en-Tourmont will take a couple of hours.

Anyone exploring the battlefields and cemeteries of World War I will want to visit Péronne's **Historial de la Grande Guerre** (www.historial. fr; Apr–Sept daily 9.30am–6pm, Oct–Mar Thu–Tue 9.30am–5pm), a museum that gives an excellent overview of the war.

Amiens

The capital of Picardy, **Amiens** ❾ is renowned for its monumental **Cathédrale Notre-Dame** (www.cathedrale-amiens.fr; Apr–Sept 8.30–6.30pm, Oct–Mar 8.30–5.30pm), a masterpiece of French Gothic architecture. Its construction was almost completed in just 44 years in the mid-13th century and as a result it has a homogeneous architectural style.

Gabled mansions in Arras

The largest cathedral in the country, it is fêted for its statues, bas-reliefs and the 16th-century oak carving of the 110 choir stalls. Dramatically depicting over 400 scenes from the Old and New Testaments, 3,650 figures present a pageant of the customs and costumes of François I's time.

Amiens' other attractions include the canalside **St-Leu** quarter, the Hortillonages – an area of water gardens east of the cathedral that is only accessible by punt or on foot – and the **Musée de Picardie** (48 rue de la République; Tue–Fri 9.30–6pm, Sat–Sun 11–6pm), with its fine collection, notably El Greco's *Portrait of a Man*, a self-portrait of Quentin de La Tour and Boucher's erotic nymphs.

COMPIÈGNE

Some 80km (50 miles) up the *autoroute du Nord* from Paris, **Compiègne** is another classical Ile-de-France royal hunting forest and palace. In addition to being Marie-Antoinette's last home, the **palace** (http://

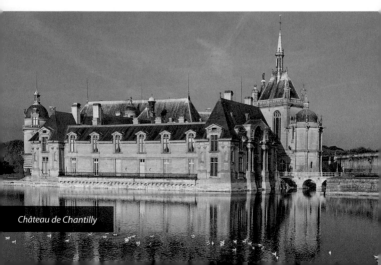

Château de Chantilly

chateaudecompiegne.fr; Wed–Mon 10am–6pm) was a favourite haunt of Napoleon III and his wife Eugénie, whose extravagant memorabilia constitute the **Musée du Second-Empire**.

Also in the palace is a fascinating **Musée de la Voiture** (Car Museum). It displays all kinds of vehicles, from the coach that carried Napoleon to Moscow in 1812 to a splendid four-horsepower Renault car from 1904 and other four-wheeled classics. At the time of writing, part of the museum was closed for restoration.

The **Forest of Compiègne** offers plenty of good walking; or, if you prefer to ride, you can hire a horse at the village of St-Jean-aux-Bois. The forest is famous for its **Clairière de l'Armistice**, where, in Marshal Foch's private railway carriage, the Germans signed the Armistice that marked their defeat in 1918. Twenty-two years later, Hitler obliged the French to sign their capitulation in the same place.

SENLIS

Just 10km (6 miles) east of Chantilly is the town of Senlis, with its imposing Gothic **cathedral** and handsome 15th- and 16th-century houses, still partly encircled by Gallo-Roman ramparts. The finely sculpted porch on the cathedral's western façade inspired the design for Chartres and Paris's Notre-Dame.

Take time to stroll along the narrow streets in the old town stretching downhill from the cathedral, which offer a combination of historic charm and modern French sophistication.

CHANTILLY

Although **Chantilly** ❿ is synonymous with the unusual quartet of whipped cream, lacemaking, porcelain and horse-racing, the biggest crowd-puller here (on non-race days, at least) is the town's magnificent château, 50km (30 miles) north of Paris. The **château** (www.chateaudechantilly.com; late Mar–late Oct daily 10am–6pm, late Oct–late Mar Wed–Mon 10.30am–5pm, closed for around two weeks in Jan), which belonged to the powerful Condé dynasty in the 17th century, consists of a reconstruction of the great edifice destroyed in the Revolution – the Grand Château – joined to the lovely, authentic Renaissance building – the Petit Château.

The main body of the château houses the **Musée Condé**, a superb collection of Italian, French and Dutch masters, including works by Raphael, Fra Angelico, Poussin and Watteau, and portraits by Clouet, Van Dyck and Teniers. One of the attractions of the collection is that the paintings are hung not in any classical order but according to the whim of their last owner, the Duke of Aumale.

The palace grounds are a pleasant place for a walk, especially the English Garden behind the Petit Château. Louis XIV was envious of the water features designed here by André Le Nôtre and insisted the master gardener do even better at Versailles. Boat trips and hot-air balloon rides are available in the park – both offer good views of the château and its park.

In June, the **Hippodrome**, west of the château, is host to the prestigious Prix du Jockey Club horse race. The **Musée Vivant du Cheval** (Equestrian Museum) is housed in the **Grandes Ecuries** (former royal stables), within 10 minutes' walk of the château; a horse show is staged daily in summer. The stables are impressive – according to popular belief their instigator, Louis-Henri, Duke of Bourbon (1692–1740), was convinced that he would be reincarnated as a horse and so undertook to build a future home fit for an equestrian king.

CHAMPAGNE-ARDENNES

Wine lovers flock to this northernmost of France's wine-producing regions, where a unique combination of geology, topography and climate has produced the world's most celebrated wine. In addition to sampling the products of the cellar masters, visitors will find gourmet meals, historic towns and dense forests.

Reims

A centre of production of the 'wine of kings', **Reims** ⓫ is also home to the cathedral where kings of France were crowned from the Middle Ages to the early 19th century. The magnificently proportioned 13th-century **Cathédrale Notre-Dame** (www.cathedrale-reims.com; daily 7.30am–7.30pm) was badly damaged in World War I, but it has been well restored and remains one of the country's greatest Gothic edifices. Try to view it in the late-afternoon sun, armed with a pair of binoculars to study the rich sculpture of the Gallery of Kings high above the windows.

Veuve-Clicquot cellars in Reims

In the interior, the most noteworthy of the surviving 13th-century **stained-glass windows** are the rose window above the western entrance, illustrating the life of the Virgin, and the one devoted to the Creation in the north arm of the transept. Directly beyond the altar is the **Chagall chapel**, in which the Russian artist connects his Jewish origins to the Christian religion with a window depicting Abraham and Jesus.

The originals of the cathedral's major sculptures are on display next door in the museum of the archbishop's residence, the **Palais du Tau** (www.palais-du-tau.fr; Tue–Sun early May–early Sept 9.30am–6.30pm, early Sept–early Mar 9.45am–12.30pm, 2–5.15pm). The most famous pieces on show are the **Smiling Angel**, symbol of Reims' hospitality, and the allegorical figure of the Synagogue, blindfolded because it was felt that the Jews were too stubborn to behold the truth of Christianity.

The city's **Champagne cellars** are in fact 250km (155 miles) of galleries quarried out of the city's chalk foundations back in the days of Roman Gaul. Practically all the major Champagne labels offer tours; the **Office de Tourisme** (beside the cathedral, at 6 rue Rockefeller) is the best source of information on hours and prices. Bear in mind that free samples are not always given at the end of visits, and that the Champagne houses may not be the cheapest places to buy Champagne.

Epernay

This town's advantage over Reims is that you can combine a visit to its cellars with a drive southward along the great **Côte des Blancs vineyards** that produce the white chardonnay grapes. The prettiest view of the vines and the Marne Valley is just 10km (6 miles) down the D10 at Cramant.

Also out of town, you can see a reconstitution of Dom Pérignon's famous 17th-century cellar and laboratory in the abbey museum of **Hautvillers**, 6km (4 miles) north of Epernay.

Troyes

The historic centre of **Troyes** ⑫ features nine Gothic churches, narrow winding streets with medieval half-timbered houses and a major

The vineyards and villages of Alsace

collection of modern art. Among the most notable churches are the **Cathédrale St-Pierre-et-St-Paul**, which took centuries to complete; the **Eglise St-Nizier**, recognisable by its gaudy tiled roof; and the **Basilique St-Urbain**. The **Musée d'Art Moderne** (Tue–Sun 10am–6pm; until 9.30pm on Thursdays), on place St-Pierre, includes a collection of paintings from 1850 to 1950.

LORRAINE

A region of strategic importance guarding the eastern approaches to Paris, Lorraine has long been a pawn in France's perennial conflicts with Germany. **Verdun** was the site of a major battle in World War I and was badly damaged by bombing in 1944. Amid the devastations of war and the more-recent depression of the region's declining coal, iron and steel industries, the historic town of Nancy stands out as a gleaming survivor. Its golden 18th-century architecture makes it a rewarding stopover (now just 90 minutes by TGV from Paris) on any journey to Alsace.

Nancy

Nancy ⓭ owes its much of its classical beauty to King Stanislas Leszczynski of Poland. Deposed by the Russians in 1736, Stanislas had the good fortune to be Louis XV's father-in-law and was given the Duchy of Lorraine as compensation. Nancy's **place Stanislas** is one of the most harmonious urban spaces in Europe.

The square's grand, spacious effect is completed to the north by a triumphal arch (dedicated to Louis XV) at the entrance to the long **place de la Carrière** – also graced by 18th-century mansions and Jean Lamour's iron grilles. At the end of the *place* – in grande rue – a splendid Renaissance doorway is all that remains of the former glory of the old ducal palace. Inside, the **Musée Historique Lorrain** (www.musee-lorrain.nancy.fr; closed for renovation) offers a fascinating glimpse of Nancy before Stanislas' time. The **Musée des Beaux-Arts** (musee-des-beaux-arts.nancy.fr; Wed–Mon 10am–6pm) at 3 place Stanislas, has a good collection of European art – notably Tintoretto, Ruysdael, Van Goyen, Ribera and Rubens, with the French represented by Delacroix, Courbet, Bonnard and Manet.

Visitors suffering from a surfeit of culture will find a change of pace at the zoo in the **Parc de la Pépinière**.

Metz

To the north of Nancy is **Metz**, the capital city of the Lorraine region and hard up against borders of both German and Luxembourg; it has been strongly influenced by German culture due to its location and history. With some striking architecture reflecting German and French style and a stunning cathedral, Metz is now home to the **Centre Pompidou-Metz** (www.centrepompidou-metz.fr; Wed–Mon 10am–6pm, Apr-Oct Fri–Sun until 7pm), the largest exhibition space outside Paris. Able to draw from some 65,000 works of modern art from the Paris centre, this gallery is bringing art to a whole new audience.

ALSATIAN STORKS

Storks are a traditional symbol of Alsace. Their population had dwindled from thousands of birds at the beginning of the 20th century to a mere couple of pairs by the early 1980s. Factors underlying this depopulation included draining of their swampy habitat and danger from electric cables in northern Europe, as well as hunting of storks and increased use of insecticides in their winter homes in Africa.

In an effort to reintroduce the birds, breeding programmes have worked to curb their migratory efforts and keep them in France over the winter. These have been so successful that by the end of 1998, more than 200 stork couples were nesting in Alsace.

The Parc des Cigognes et des Loutres in Hunawihr is home to around 150 storks and you can walk through acres of stork habitat and also see otters swimming, feeding and playing.

ALSACE

One of the reasons why the Germans and the French have fought for possession of this province is that it's such a good place to live. Rich farmland, vineyards and dense forest, with the protective Vosges mountain range on one side and the great Rhine river on the other, combine to make Alsace a wonderful self-contained and rich region. Changes of nationality have left Alsace with a distinctive

Strasbourg Cathedral

dialect, architecture, cuisine and local pride – the best of both worlds. Visitors can choose to stay in cosmopolitan Strasbourg, picturesque Colmar or hillside villages, and can eat in cosy *winstubs* (wine bars) or stylish restaurants.

Strasbourg

This intellectual, cultural and economic centre has emerged handsome, if not unscathed, from its turbulent past. Many Gothic and Renaissance buildings here in **Strasbourg** ⑭ have been lovingly restored. The *winstubs* of its old neighbourhoods are gathering places for university students whose predecessors include the German writer Goethe.

It's a good town for walking the narrow streets, or for taking a **boat cruise** on the River Ill, which divides into two branches to loop the historic centre. Launches start from the Pont Ste-Madeleine behind the Château des Rohan.

The asymmetrical silhouette of the magnificent Gothic **cathedral** (www.cathedrale-strasbourg.fr; Mon–Sat 8.30–11.15am, 12.45–5.45pm, Sun 2–5.15pm), with its single tower and steeple rising on the

ern side of its facade, will give your tour of the city an inspiring
Combining the architectural style of Ile-de-France Gothic with
h German sculpture, the cathedral is an apt symbol of Alsatian
. The original designer, Erwin von Steinbach, began the pink
sandstone facade in 1277, but only got as far as the splendid
of Apostles over the central rose window.

Ulrich von Ensingen – the master builder of the great cathedral of
Ulm – began construction of the octagon of the north tower in 1399.
The graceful openwork spire was added in the 15th century by Johannes
Hültz of Cologne.

A popular attraction, situated in the southern arm of the transept
and approached through the Portail de l'Horloge, is the 19th-century
astronomical clock with its elaborate mechanical figures that appear
with chimes at 12.30pm. In the summer, arrive by noon or you won't
see a thing. After everyone's gone, stay on to see the marvellous 13th-
century sculpted **Pilier des Anges** (Angel's Pillar) in peace. Climb the

Storks are the symbols of Alsace

300 or so stairs to the platform just below the steeple for a splendid view over the city.

On place de la Cathédrale, at the beginning of rue Mercière, stands the 13th-century **Pharmacie du Cerf**, which is even older than the cathedral and is reputedly the oldest pharmacy in France. The other venerable house in the square, now a restaurant, is the **Maison Kammerzell**. The ground floor dates from 1467, and the beautifully sculpted wooden facade of the superstructure was built in 1589.

Guardian of the city's medieval and Renaissance treasures, the **Musée de l'Oeuvre Notre-Dame** (place du Chateau; www.musees.strasbourg. eu for all museums; Tue & Thu-Sun 10am–1pm 2–6pm) is itself made up of a superb group of 14th , 16th- and 17th-century houses around a secluded Gothic garden on place du Château, south of the cathedral. Besides sheltering the most vulnerable of the cathedral's statuary and stained-glass windows from the 12th-century Romanesque building, the museum has a fine collection of Alsatian medieval paintings.

In the midst of the predominantly Germanic old city centre, the **Château des Rohan**, the classical 18th-century residence that was the home of Strasbourg's princes and cardinals, makes an emphatically French statement.

The furniture collection of the château's delightful **Musée des Arts Décoratifs** (Wed and Fri–Mon 10am–1pm 2–6pm) offers interesting comparisons between Parisian and Alsatian aristocratic and bourgeois tastes of both the 17th and 18th centuries. However, the museum's pride and joy is its ceramics collection, displaying beside Europe's finest porcelain and faïence the astonishing Rococo craftsmanship of the Strasbourg Hannong family, most remarkably a huge tureen in the form of a turkey. If you didn't see the astronomical clock in the cathedral, you can have a close-up view here of figures from the original 14th-century model.

The château also houses Strasbourg's **Musée des Beaux-Arts** (Wed and Fri–Mon 10am–1pm 2–6pm), noteworthy for its Giotto *Crucifixion*, Raphael's *Portrait de Jeune Femme* and Watteau's *L'Ecureuse de cuivre*.

Alsatian cuisine

Don't limit yourself to tasting Alsace's intense dry wines – the cuisine is equally toothsome and varied. The hors d'oeuvre *tarte flambée* is the Alsatian equivalent of pizza, traditionally made with crème fraîche, cheese and onions, and baked in a wood-fired oven.

Behind the château, cross the Pont Ste-Madeleine over the Ill and stroll along the quai des Bateliers, past the remnants of old Strasbourg, to the 14th-century **place du Corbeau** near the bridge of the same name.

Continue along the quai St-Nicolas to the **Musée Alsacien** (Wed and Fri–Mon 10am–1pm 2–6pm) at No. 23, a group of 16th- and 17th-century houses appropriate to the colourful collections of Alsatian folklore. Children will love the ancient toys and dolls. Instruments of worship and ritual illustrate the religious life of the province's important Jewish community.

Make your way west to Pont St-Martin for a first view of the city's most enchanting quarter, the old tannery district known as **Petite France**. At a point where the Ill divides into four canals, the tanners shared the waterways with the millers and fishermen. Sturdy gabled houses line the des Dentelles and rue du Bain-aux-Plantes.

The **Barrage Vauban** – remains of the fortifications built by Vauban for Louis XIV – spans the Ill to the west. Its roof affords a splendid panoramic **view** across the canals and Petite France to the soaring silhouette of the cathedral. At sunset it makes the perfect finish to a day's walk, but many visitors like to start out from here and reverse the order of the walk we have proposed, reserving the cathedral for a triumphant climax.

Route du Vin

Sheltered from the cold, damp, northwest winds by the Vosges mountains, the vineyards of Alsace enjoy an ideal microclimate for producing white wines that confidently hold their own against the more acclaimed wines of Burgundy and Bordeaux.

The vineyards hug the gentle slopes between the Vosges and the Rhine Valley along a single narrow 120-km (75-mile) strip that stretches from Marlenheim, just west of Strasbourg, down to Thann, outside Mulhouse. The winding 'wine route' is well signposted; its delightful medieval and 16th-century villages and castles – such as Haut-Koenigsbourg and Kaysersberg – make it the prettiest vineyard tour in the country, best of all during the October wine harvest. Tasting and purchases are possible at many of the properties. Ask at the local *syndicat d'initiative* or Colmar's Maison du Vin d'Alsace for information about the vineyard tours organised from Obernai and Turckheim.

A walk around the lovely shaded ramparts of **Obernai** will convince you of the perennial prosperity of its wine growers and farmers. Among the elegant, spotless timbered houses of the 16th-century place du Marché, note the fine **Halle aux Blés** (Corn Market) and **Hôtel de Ville**, as well as the handsome Renaissance **Puits aux Six Seaux** (Six Pails Well) situated between the town hall and the parish church.

Equally famous for its Riesling wines and its Renaissance houses, picturesque **Riquewihr** is often overcrowded during the tourist season. Cars must be left at the southern end of the town. If you arrive in Riquewihr on a quiet day, have a good look at the stately 16th-century **Maison Liebrich** and at the 17th-century **Maison Preiss-Zimmer**, on the main street (rue du Général de-Gaulle).

Just before you reach the main gate and town symbol, the 13th-century **Dolder**, turn off to the right and take a peep

Riquewihr is famed for its shop signs of forged iron

at the little **ghetto** in the wooden-galleried Cour des Juifs. And for those who enjoy inspecting ancient instruments of terror and torture, there's a medieval chamber of horrors set in the **Tour des Voleurs** (Thieves' Tower).

Nestling at the foot of its ruined castle, the pretty medieval town of **Kaysersberg** is widely known as the birthplace of Nobel Peace Prize winner Albert Schweitzer (1875–1965). His parents' house is now the **Centre Culturel Schweitzer** (124 rue du Général-de-Gaulle), devoted to the life of the humanitarian, who was also a fine performer of Bach's organ works. A 10-minute walk up the wooded hill to the **castle tower** gives a view of the town and surrounding valley of the Weiss river.

Colmar

Some people make a pilgrimage to **Colmar** ⑮ with the sole purpose of visiting its great art gallery. But the town itself, with its miraculously preserved old city centre, has much else to offer. It also makes a quieter alternative to Strasbourg as a base for touring the vineyards of Alsace.

The jewel-like roof of the Hôtel-Dieu in Beaune

Converted from a 13th-century convent of Dominican nuns, the **Musée d'Unterlinden** (www.musee-unterlinden.com; Wed–Mon 9am–6pm) provides a perfect setting in which to view one of the world's undisputed masterpieces of religious art, Matthias Grünewald's awe-inspiring **Isenheim altarpiece**. Created for the Isenheim Convent of St Anthony between 1512 and 1516, the altarpiece originally folded out in three panels, which are now mounted for exhibition in separate sections. To appreciate the full impact of the whole work, view it in reverse order, starting at the far end with the stately sculpted polychrome wooden panel of saints Augustine, Anthony and Jerome, carved by Niklaus Hagenauer. The first of Grünewald's painted panels depicts on one side the conversion and temptation of Anthony and on the other the birth of Jesus and a chorus of angels. The second panel is devoted to the Annunciation and Resurrection and, on the reverse side, what is perhaps the most pain-filled and exalted portrayal of the Crucifixion ever realised. Be sure also to see the superb altarpiece of Martin Schongauer, Hans Holbein's portrait of a woman and Lucas Cranach's exquisite *Mélancolie*.

Renowned Swiss architects Herzog & de Meuron recently oversaw an ambitious, multi-year restoration and expansion project that has seen an annexe and a new building for temporary exhibitions added, doubling the museum's exhibition space in the process. The revamped museum was officially opened in January 2016 by President Francoise Hollande.

In the old town centre – which is closed to traffic – keep an eye open for the many handsome gabled houses of the Renaissance period: the **Ancienne Douane** (Old Customs House, grand-rue); **Maison des Arcades** (grand-rue); **Maison Pfister** (rue des Marchands) and **Maison des Têtes** (rue des Têtes).

The **Petite Venise** (Little Venice) district is south of the old town. From the St-Pierre bridge there is a lovely view of its flowery river banks, weeping willows and timbered houses, with the tower of St Martin's church in the distance. The district on the opposite bank of the river was once a fortified enclave, inhabited mainly by market gardeners who used to sell their wares from barges on the river. It still holds on

The birth of France

Just south of Fontenay near the village of Alise-Ste-Reine is the site of a decisive battle in French history where, as one writer put it, 'Gaul died and France was born', when Julius Caesar defeated the Gauls under Vercingétorix. A Gallo-Roman city and museum can be found nearby.

to its original name of *Krutenau* (Vegetable Waterway).

Martin Schongauer's beautiful altar painting *Vierge au Buisson de Roses* (Madonna in the Rose Bower) can be found in the **Eglise des Dominicains** (Tue and Thu–Sun 3–6pm), along with a number of remarkable 14th- and 15th-century stained-glass windows.

Colmar is also the birthplace of Auguste Bartholdi, designer of the Statue of Liberty. His 17th-century house (30 rue des Marchands) is now the **Musée Bartholdi** (www.musee-bartholdi.fr; Mar–Dec Tue–Sun 10am–noon, 2–6pm), displaying his models and drawings. His statue of Napoleon's General Jean Rapp, another local resident, can be seen on the place Rapp.

BURGUNDY

The prosperous Burgundy region has a great variety of attractions: fine wines and food, canal holidays on the area's waterways, drifting past green meadows, Romanesque architecture, tiny villages with exquisite parish churches and open-air stone laundries, the grand ducal palace in Dijon, the Hospices in Beaune and the Unesco-protected World Heritage sites of Vézelay and Fontenay. If you are driving from Paris, you'll get the best out of Burgundy by leaving the *autoroute* at either the Courtenay or the Auxerre exit and travelling the rest of the way on the excellent – and scenic – secondary roads.

Auxerre

Overlooking the Yonne river and with several interesting churches and an astronomical clock, **Auxerre** ⑯ makes a good first stop for trips into the Burgundy interior, particularly if you want to stock up for a picnic. It is the main distribution point for the famous Chablis white wines, but you may prefer to drive out to the vineyards in the delightful country-side east of the *autoroute*.

Vallée du Serein

This is just one out of a score of leisurely backroad trips you can make through northern Burgundy's meandering green valleys. Either cutting across from **Tonnerre** or starting out from the village of Chablis, follow the course of the Serein river (a tributary of the Yonne) towards Avallon.

Noyers is a fortified medieval village with 16 towers in its ramparts. Many of its timbered-and-gabled houses date back to the 14th and 15th centuries, notably in place de l'Hôtel-de-Ville and rue du Poids-du-Roy. From the Renaissance church, there's a pretty view over the river.

At **L'Isle-sur-Serein**, the river divides to encircle the town and the ruins of its 15th-century château. Leave the river briefly to loop east around

Burgundy landscape

Café du Centre in Cluny

Talcy, with its Romanesque church and the 13th-century château of Thizy, before ending your trip at **Montréal.** This medieval town has a Gothic church with a Renaissance interior; note the Nottingham alabaster altarpiece.

Abbaye de Fontenay

This magnificent, Unesco protected Cistercian **abbey** (www. abbayedefontenay.com; daily Apr–Nov 10am–6pm, mid-Nov–late Mar 10am–noon and 2–5pm) is around 6km (4 miles) from Montbard, and is set behind high walls in a lovely valley at the edge of a forest. Founded in the early 12th century by St Bernard, it includes a church, cloisters, scriptorium, refectory, sleeping quarters, infirmary, forge, bakery and herb garden – everything for a self-sufficient community. The building was converted into a paper mill in the 19th century, but has since been restored and the cloisters once again present the calm and simplicity that were the ideals of its founder. It is often the setting for classical music concerts in the summer.

As you go through the gate decorated with the arms of the Cistercian order, you'll notice a niche for a guard dog below the staircase. On the right is an austere hostel and chapel for the few pilgrims who passed this way and beyond it lies the forge of the hard-working Cistercians. To the left of the entrance are the monks' bakery and a surprisingly imposing pigeon loft.

Paid for by Bishop Everard of Norwich, for whom Fontenay was a refuge from the hostility of Henry II of England, the **abbey church** has a sober, unadorned beauty, although it lacks a belltower, as there were no distant faithful to be called to worship. The interior has harmonious proportions and fine acoustics because St Bernard was a great lover of music. A serene 13th-century statue of the Virgin Mary stands in the northern arm of the transept.

Vézelay

A centre of spirituality in a beautiful rustic setting, **Vézelay** ⑰ is the home of one of the major churches on the pilgrim route from Germany and the Netherlands to Santiago de Compostela in Spain. Today it welcomes tourists, in large numbers. If you're travelling at the height of the tourist season, it is vital to make an early start to avoid the worst of the crowds.

To recapture something of the experience of the medieval pilgrim, park at place du Champ-de-Foire, pass through the turreted Porte Neuve, and follow the **Promenade des Fossés**, which takes you along the ancient ramparts lined with walnut trees.

At the Porte Ste-Croix, there is a magnificent view over the Cure river valley and the path that leads to the place where, in 1146, St Bernard urged King Louis VII to lead the French on the Second Crusade. This was also to be the starting point of the Third Crusade in 1190, when England's Richard the Lion-Heart joined forces with Philippe Auguste.

Vézelay's **Basilique Ste-Madeleine** (www.basiliquede vezelay.org; daily 7am–8pm, Mon from 8am; no visits during services; free), with its repository of relics of Mary Magdalene, is a magnificent

Romanesque Basilique Ste-Madeleine, Vézelay

example of French Romanesque architecture, in spite of the damage inflicted by natural disasters, wars and revolution. The 19th-century restorations of the renowned architect Viollet-le-Duc have maintained the church's majestic harmony.

The narthex, or entrance hall to the nave, is crowned by a magnificent sculpted **tympanum** of Jesus enthroned after the Resurrection, preaching his message to the Apostles. On the central supporting pillar is a statue of John the Baptist – beheaded not by Herod but by iconoclastic Huguenot vandals.

The nave is a wonder of light and lofty proportions, enhanced by the luminous beige stone and the splendid ribbed vaulting. In contrast to the exalted quality of the tympanum's sculpture, the robust carvings of the **capitals** in the nave are lively and down-to-earth, making a clearly popular appeal to the throngs of visiting pilgrims.

The themes depicted on the capitals are from the Bible and the legends of the saints. Beside David and Goliath, Daniel in the lions' den, and the building of Noah's ark, one sculpture shows the corrupting influence of dancing while another shows St Eugenia, tonsured and disguised as a monk, opening her robe to convince a sceptical friar that she's a woman.

On the tree-shaded **terrace** beyond the basilica, relax on one of the benches and enjoy the splendid view looking out over the forested plateau of the Morvan. Then explore the old houses, wells and courtyards in the town's narrow lanes leading back down to the place du Champ-de-Foire.

Autun

At the other end of the densely wooded Morvan plateau, the town of Autun has been an administrative centre since Augustus defeated the Gauls, and its quadruple arched gates and 15,000 capacity amphitheatre bear witness to its imperial past.

Medieval prosperity left behind the 12th-century **Cathédrale St-Lazare** (daily 9am–7pm; free). On the tympanum of the central portal, note the rich carving of Jesus presiding at the Last Judgment.

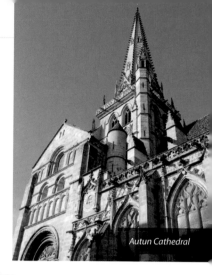
Autun Cathedral

On the left are the happy few being welcomed by St Peter. Immediately to the right of Jesus is the weighing of the souls, with St Michael trying to stop Satan from cheating. On the far right, a cauldron is boiling a few of the unlucky ones. Below Jesus' feet is a Latin inscription that suggests that the tympanum was the work of Gislebertus (Gilbert). It says: *Gislebertus did this. May such terror terrify those in thrall to earthly error, for the horror of these images tells what awaits them.*

Gilbert is also believed to have carved the magnificent **capitals** topping the pillars of the nave and aisles, and some of the more fragile pieces are exhibited in an upstairs **chapter room**. The sculpture places a graphic emphasis on the ugliness of sin (the hanging of Judas, the devil tempting Jesus) and the simple beauty of virtue.

At the nearby **Musée Rolin** (temporarily closed) there is a fine collection of Burgundian and Flemish painting and sculpture. The museum is partly housed in the elegant 15th-century mansion that belonged to Nicolas Rolin, a wealthy dignitary and the benefactor of the Hôtel-Dieu at Beaune (see page 113).

Dijon

The capital of Burgundy and a centre of art, architecture, culture and learning, **Dijon** ⑱ is just one hour from Paris by TGV. The ideal gateway for a tour of the vineyards to the south or a drive around the pretty Val-Suzon to the north, it's also a good starting point for cruises on the Canal de Bourgogne.

One of the attractions of the city itself are the streets around place Darcy, dominated by an Arc de Triomphe, and Dijon's main thoroughfare rue de la Liberté, where you can hunt for such regional delicacies as mustard (look out for the historic Maille shop), *pain d'épices* (a honey-sweetened, aniseed-flavoured gingerbread) and crème de cassis, the blackcurrant liqueur that transforms white wine into a refreshing *kir*. (The drink is named after a former mayor of Dijon, Félix Kir; a true kir is made with a white aligoté de Bourgogne.) For wines you may want to wait for your tour of the vineyards or the wider selection available at Beaune. Take a break in place Darcy or on place François Rude, half-way down rue de la Liberté; the square is named after the sculptor, a local lad, whose most famous work is probably *La Marseillaise*, on the Arc de Triomphe in Paris.

Dijon is a great city to explore on foot. To see some of the town's past glories, head for the semi-circular place de la Libération (formerly place Royale), designed by Jules Hardouin-Mansart. The elegant 17th- and 18th-century facades of the **Palais des Ducs** conceal the underlying Renaissance structures of the dukes' heyday, but many of their treasures remain to be seen inside, in the **Musée des Beaux-Arts** (beaux-arts.dijon.fr; both Wed–Mon, Jun–Sep 10am–6.30pm, Oct–May 9.30am–6pm).

You get a notion of the magnificence of Burgundian court life by starting your visit with the **ducal kitchens**, built in 1435, which boast six enormous walk-in cooking hearths. Highlights include a model of the old palace and a collection of Burgundian sculpture from the 15th century to the present day. In the picture galleries, the dukes' close links with the Flemish masters of their day are illustrated by works such as the fine *Nativité* of the anonymous Maître de Flémalle and Dierick Bouts's *Tête de Christ*. The collection also includes works by Rubens, Frans Hals, Veronese, Konrad Witz and Martin Schongauer.

But the museum's greatest treasures are the dukes' tombs in the **Salle des Gardes**. It took the sculptors Jean de Marville, Claus Sluter and Claus de Werve 26 years (1385–1411) to complete the intricate marble and alabaster sculptures for the extravagant **mausoleum of Philippe le Hardi**. On the sides of the tomb bearing the recumbent statue of the duke are carved 41 expressive figures of mourners cloaked in monastic capes. The double sepulchre of Jean sans Peur and his wife, Marguerite de Bavière, is also lavishly sculpted, although more stylised. Near the ducal tombs is Rogier van der Weyden's portrait of the third great duke, Philippe le Bon, with the Golden Fleece – the emblem of the chivalrous order that he founded in 1429.

Maille – one of the best brands of Dijon mustard

To the east of the palace are the Eglise St-Etienne and Eglise St-Michel. To the north are the 13th-century Gothic Notre-Dame and rue de la Chouette (named after the owl sculpture – *chouette* means owl – on the northern side of Notre-Dame). This street leads to rue Verrerie, home to attractive late-Gothic and Renaissance houses, with picturesque inner courtyards, many of which have been transformed into antiques shops. In rue des Forges, note the **Hôtel Chambellan** (at No. 34) and the **Hôtel Aubriot** (at No. 40), home of the Provost of Paris who built the Bastille prison.

Route des Grands Crus

Delightful as the vineyards of Burgundy may be, the landscape and villages of certain other *routes des vins* may be considered prettier – those of Alsace, for instance. And other wine growers, such as those around Bordeaux, may have more handsome châteaux. But none can compete with the reputations of the famed names of the Côte d'Or (*côte* here means hillside,

The famed wines of the Côte d'Or

not coast), which make a wine connoisseur's taste buds tingle: Gevrey-Chambertin, Chambolle-Musigny, Vougeot, Vosne-Romanée, Nuits-St-Georges, Pommard, Meursault, Puligny-Montrachet and Santenay.

From Dijon down to Santenay, the Côte d'Or is just 60km (37 miles) long. As you drive south from Dijon, be sure to get off the main road, the D974 (sometimes still referred to as the N74), onto the parallel D122, signposted as the **Route des Grands Crus** (Route of the Great Vintages). You then eventually rejoin the D974 at Clos de Vougeot.

The sign *'Grappillage Interdit'* means just what it says – 'Don't steal the grapes'; it refers even to those left hanging at the end of the harvest. Many of the famous vineyards are open to visitors, but tasting is strictly for customers who show an intention to buy.

The village of **Gevrey-Chambertin** and the medieval château's wine cellars make a good first stop. But the best cellars open to the public are those in the château at **Clos de Vougeot** (www.closdevougeot.fr), owned by the Cistercian monks until the Revolution and now the property of the Chevaliers du Tastevin (fraternity of wine tasters). The splendid old vats and winepresses are themselves worth the visit, and the guides will tell you everything you want to know about wine.

Beaune

For the beginner – and for many others, too – **Beaune** ⑲ is the place to buy. It's the centre of the industry and practically all the great wines are represented here. You won't get a better bargain at the vineyard unless you know the owner. A little **Musée du Vin** (www.beaune.fr/culture-et-loisirs/musees/musee-du-vin-de-bourgogne; rue d'Enfer; Wed–Mon 10am–1pm, 2–6pm closed in winter) tells the history of wine making, with all its paraphernalia, from Roman times to the present day.

Beaune's most prized building, the **Hôtel-Dieu**, is a beautifully preserved 15th-century hospital with spectacular coloured roof tiles. Be sure to see the masterpiece of Flemish art commissioned for the hospital chapel, Rogier van der Weyden's altarpiece of the **Last Judgment**. It is now on display in the museum (daily Apr–Nov 9am–6.30pm, Dec–Mar shorter hours), along with tapestries that adorned the walls of the unheated hospital wards to keep the patients warm. The annual wine auction every November is still the high point in the local wine calendar.

Chalon-sur-Saône

Half-timbered houses still crowd around the Cathédrale St-Vincent in **Chalon-sur-Saône** to the south of Beaune. The town was the birthplace of Nicéphore Niépce, the inventor of photography, and has a museum dedicated to him (www.museeniepce.com; Wed–Mon July–Aug 10am–1pm 2–6pm, Sept–June 9.30–11.45am, 2–5.45pm; free).

Cluny

The abbey (52km/32miles south of Chalon) that now stands in ruins at the southern tip of Burgundy ruled its medieval world in the same way that Louis XIV's Versailles dominated 17th-century France. In fact, the vast 12th-century **Abbatiale St-Pierre-et-St-Paul** (www.cluny-abbaye.fr; daily Apr–Sept 9.30am–6pm, Oct–Mar 9.30am–5pm) was the largest church in Christendom until the completion of St Peter's in Rome in the 17th century. Only the right arm of one of the two transepts and the octagonal belltower, the **Clocher de l'Eau-Bénite**, remain. But these are

WITH A WHIMPER NOT A BANG

Founded in 910, Benedictine Abbey Cluny organised the first Crusades and masterminded the pilgrimages to Santiago de Compostela. Its abbots were emperors. At the beginning of the 12th century, it ruled more than 1,450 monastic institutions with 10,000 monks in France, Spain, Italy, Germany and Britain. The abbey's destruction began in 1798, not by revolutionary iconoclasts hell-bent on revenge for centuries of exploitation, but by a merchant from nearby Mâcon. He bought the abbey for 2,000,000 francs and systematically dismantled it over a period of 25 years – in order to build a set of national riding stables.

impressive in themselves, and Cluny's excellent young guides (English-speaking in summer) will help you to imagine the rest. Originally, there were five naves, two transepts, five bell-towers and 225 choir stalls.

The elegant classical 18th-century **cloisters** make a poignant contrast with the Romanesque church. The 13th-century **granary**, beside an even older flour mill, is now a **museum** for the abbey's sculpted capitals displayed on reconstructed pillars.

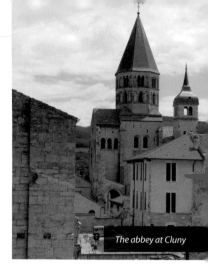

The abbey at Cluny

To see Cluny's impact on the surrounding countryside, visit a few of the villages whose Romanesque churches were constructed by Cluny's architects and craftsmen: among them, St-Vincent-des-Prés, Berzé-la-Ville, Malay and Taizé, a famous Christian pilgrimage site.

THE JURA

The Jura mountains cover several eastern *départements* making up the region of Franche-Comté. The rampart-like mountains and dense pine forests keep this area remote and, even today, blessedly unspoiled. This area is a favourite of hikers who enjoy invigorating journeys through dense forests and along the river valleys celebrated in the paintings of Gustave Courbet.

Besançon

A convenient base for detours, the capital of the Franche-Comté region, **Besançon ⑳**, has an attractive city centre around the pedestrian zone of the **Grande-Rue**. Favourite sons of Besançon include Victor Hugo, 19th-century thinker Pierre-Joseph Proudhon, and Auguste and Louis

Lumière, inventors of cinematography. Guided tours are available by boat and audio guides can be rented at the Office de Tourisme on place de la Première Armée Française.

The city is renowned for its **citadel** (www.citadelle.com; daily Apr–July, Sept–Oct 9am–6pm, July–Aug 9am–7pm, Nov–Dec Feb-Mar 10am–5pm, closed Jan), built by Vauban. The fortress offers good views and houses several museums, including the **Musée Comtoise** full of local artefacts; an Insectarium; an Aquarium; and a Noctarium, an exhibit of local nocturnal animals. The harrowing Musée de la Résistance et de la Déportation is not suitable for young children. The **Porte Noire**, a Roman arch on rue de la Convention, leads you to the 12th-century **Cathédrale St-Jean**. Try to visit the cathedral's **astronomical clock** on the hour to see the figures emerge from the clock.

The **Musée des Beaux-Arts** (www.mbaa.besancon.fr; Sat–Sun 10am–6pm, Mon and Wed–Fri: Apr–Oct 10am–12.30pm 2–6pm, Nov–Mar 2–6pm), in place de la Révolution, is claimed to be the oldest in France

Normandy fields

(1694). Of the Italian paintings, Bellini's *L'Ivresse de Noé* (The Drunkenness of Noah) is outstanding. Look, too, for Cranach's *La Nymphe à la Source* and fine French works by Bonnard and Rodin.

Arc-et-Senans

The 18th-century **Saline Royale** (Royal Saltworks; www.salineroyale. com; daily, July–Aug 9am–7pm, Apr–June and Sept–Oct 9am–6pm, Nov–Mar 10am–noon, 2–5pm), now abandoned, is surely one of the most elegant factories in the world. It was in fact the nucleus of a utopian city conceived by Claude-Nicolas Ledoux, who had the outlandish idea of making working conditions for the salt-labourers pleasant.

In green surroundings, the buildings of the saltworks are set in a semicircle around administrative offices in simple classical style. There is a **museum** devoted to Ledoux's avant-garde theories and seminars are held here on urban and industrial planning.

Vallée de la Loue

While in the Jura, trace the Loue river and its tributary, the Lison, back to their cascading **sources** through the landscapes that inspired so many of Gustave Courbet's paintings. His home town was **Ornans**. Stand on the Grand Pont for the celebrated view of the strange old timbered houses reflected in the river that runs through the town. Close by the bridge is the **Musée Courbet** (www.musee-courbet.fr; Wed–Mon Apr–June 10am–noon, 2–6pm, July–Sept 10am–6pm, Oct–Mar 9am–noon, 2–5pm), set in the artist's childhood home.

Les Reculées

These intriguing horseshoe-shaped valleys nestle like narrow amphitheatres against abrupt rocky cliffs, making rewarding destinations for a day's hike. One of the best is the **Cirque de Baume**, between Lons-le-Saunier and Baume-les-Messieurs. Southeast of Arbois, the **Reculée des Planches** leads to the fairytale waterfalls of the Cuisance and ends at the dramatic **Cirque du Fer à Cheval**.

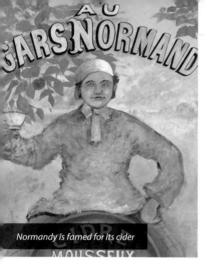

Normandy is famed for its cider

THE NORTHWEST

Northwestern France includes a long sea coast, stretching along the English Channel (*La Manche*) around Brittany and down to the mouth of the Loire. The sea has always played an important role in the history of this region, from Scandinavians arriving in longships to Celts fleeing Anglo-Saxons and Normans invading England.

Normandy's coastline is dotted with old seaside resorts, such wonders as Mont-St-Michel and reminders of the Allied invasions of World War II. The interior is a patchwork of rich green farmland, timber-framed houses, ruined abbeys, Romanesque churches and busy cities. The cuisine is distinctive, featuring apples, butter, cream and cheese. Brittany's countryside is wilder, with a jagged coastline to match. But the rugged coast shelters sandy beaches, seaside resorts and fishing ports, and inland are picturesque châteaux and towns, canals and rivers. The Loire Valley is impressive for more than its many châteaux. Its coastline, waterways, forests, architecture, wine and food present the good life in abundant variety.

NORMANDY

This region divides into an eastern half, Haute-Normandie, along the Seine Valley and similar in scenery to the Ile-de-France; and the more rugged Basse-Normandie to the west, more akin to neighbouring Brittany. Vast expanses of land are cultivated; orchards and lush cattle pastures produce the famous strong cider and pungent cheeses. The

Atlantic climate produces changeable but pleasant summer weather. Visitors should be wary of incoming tides, which can move very fast.

Dieppe

As France's oldest seaside resort and the closest beach to Paris, **Dieppe** ㉑ is a popular gateway to Normandy for those crossing the English Channel from Newhaven. But as a working fishing port with a pretty seafront, long promenade and restored 17th-century St-Jacques quarter, the town is worth a visit in its own right.

Children will enjoy the **Cité de la Mer** (37 rue de l'Asile Thomas; www.estrancitedelamer.fr; Mon–Sat 9.30am–6pm Sun 9.30am–12.30pm 1.30–6pm), with exhibits on the history of boatbuilding, the fishing industry, and how tides and currents have shaped the coastline.

The **Musée de Dieppe** (Wed–Mon June–Sept daily 10am–6pm, Oct–May 10am–noon, 2–5pm, Sun until 6pm), also known as the Château-Musée, in the 15th-century château in rue de Chastes, has an excellent collection of model ships and carvings in ivory, dating back to the 18th century, when elephant tusks were among the major imports from Africa and Asia.

Memorials in square du Canada and the beautifully kept Canadian Cemetery in nearby **Hautot-sur-Mer** commemorate the courageous

CIDER, CALVADOS, CHEESE AND CREAM

The four Cs of Normandy are evident everywhere in the region – in the landscape full of orchards and dairy cattle, on the signs offering *Ici Vente Cidre* (Cider for Sale) and on the dinner table.

The cider available is both alcoholic and non-alcoholic. Calvados – an apple brandy – is not always reserved for the end of the meal but is sipped between courses to cleanse the palate.

Among the fine cheeses you'll find in the region are Camembert, Livarot, Neufchâtel and Pont l'Evêque.

but abortive Canadian raid on German-held Dieppe on 19 August 1942.

Rouen

Rouen 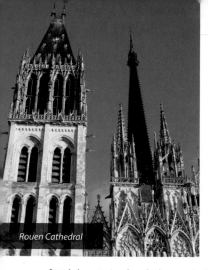 is the ancient centre of Normandy's thriving textile industry and the place of Joan of Arc's martyrdom – a national symbol of resistance to tyranny. The writer Gustave Flaubert was born in Rouen and set his masterpiece *Madame Bovary* here.

Rouen Cathedral

Normandy's capital suffered devastating bomb damage in 1944, and many buildings have since been lovingly restored or reconstructed. The beautiful medieval and Renaissance centre around the cathedral has been renovated and pedestrianised. Rouen continues to work on its monuments and public buildings, and quayside renovations have brought life back to the riverside with new promenades.

To tour the centre of the city, start your walk at the western end of the historic district, on **place du Vieux-Marché**. The old and new Rouen come together around the bright and airy market halls and the attractive modern **Eglise Ste-Jeanne-d'Arc**. Inside the church are some fine 16th-century **stained-glass windows**, salvaged from an older church bombed in 1944. Nearby is a monument to mark the spot where Joan was burned at the stake in 1431.

Leading eastward from the market is Rouen's most famous street, **rue du Gros-Horloge** – now as always the city's bustling commercial centre. Its timber-framed houses of the 15th, 16th and 17th centuries are marvellous examples of sturdy Norman architecture, achieving a pleasing irregularity with the plaster set in oblique forms between the solid oak posts and collar beams supporting the balconies. The elegant Renaissance arched clocktower of the **Gros Horloge** is Rouen's emblem. The ornamental gilded clock face has only one hand, for the hours.

East of the Gros Horloge stands the great **Cathédrale Notre-Dame** (www.cathedrale-rouen.net; Mon 2–6pm, Tue–Fri 9am–noon 2–6pm, Sat 9am–6pm, Sun 8am–6pm; free), made famous in modern times by Monet's many Impressionist studies of its facade. The asymmetry of the two towers embracing the delicate tracery of the slender spires creates a distinctive silhouette.

The cathedral was constructed over several centuries, and the facade offers a remarkably harmonious anthology of Gothic architecture. The north tower, the **Tour St-Romain**, has the sober simplicity of the cathedral's early Gothic beginnings in the 12th century, while the taller, more elaborate south tower, the **Tour de Beurre**, is in the Flamboyant Gothic style of the 15th century. According to local belief, Catholic burghers subsidised this 'Butter Tower' in return for the privilege of eating Normandy butter during Lent.

The austerely sculpted porches flanking the main entrance are from the early period, and the more ornamental elongated central porch and the gabled upper windows were added in the 15th and 16th centuries. The main spire is neo-Gothic from the 19th century.

The rather severe interior of the cathedral contrasts with its elaborate exterior, but the impact of the double-storeyed nave is lightened by the tall arches of the choir. In the Chapelle de la Vierge

Half-timbered house in Rouen

Sun worship

In 1919 German doctors discovered that certain deficiency diseases in children could be alleviated by exposure to sunlight. It began the sun worship that made resorts out of deserts and turned once-grand towns such as Deauville into evocative relics from a bygone age.

(beyond the choir) is the monumental Renaissance **Tomb of the Cardinals of Amboise**, with superbly sculpted allegories of the cardinal virtues. On the south side of the choir is the more modest tomb of the most heroic of medieval English kings, the 12th-century crusader portrayed recumbent above the inscription in Latin: *Here is buried the heart of King Richard of England, known as the Lion-Heart.*

Behind the cathedral, cross over rue de la République to the 15th-century **Eglise St-Maclou** (Apr–Sep Mon, Sat, Sun 10am–noon, 2–6pm, Oct–Mar until 5.30pm; free), the richest example of Flamboyant Gothic in the country. Note the masterful Renaissance carving of the oak doors on the central and north portals. In the interior, the same exuberant artistry can be admired in the sculpted wood organ frame and the stone tracery of the **spiral staircase**.

Turn north onto rue Damiette, graced by some of the town's handsomest houses. The street leads to the elegant 14th-century Gothic abbey church, the **Abbatiale St-Ouen**, best observed from the little park east of the chancel.

The last great monument of the old town, in rue aux Juifs, is the grand **Palais de Justice**, a jewel of Renaissance and Flamboyant Gothic architecture built on the site of the medieval ghetto. Excavations have uncovered a 12th-century structure under part of the palace. This structure is known as the **Monument Juif**, although experts are still debating whether it was a synagogue, a school or a private residence.

This prosperous city has many museums, including a well-endowed **Musée des Beaux-Arts** (mbarouen.fr; square Verdrel; Wed–Mon

10am–6pm), with works by Velázquez, Caravaggio, Perugino, Veronese and Rubens. French painters represented include Delacroix and François Clouet, as well as Géricault, who was born in Rouen. The **Musée de la Céramique** (1 rue Faucon; museedelaceramique.fr; Wed–Mon 2–6pm; free) displays the local colourful glazed earthenware and china from France and the rest of the world. For a collection of early – and attention-grabbing – medical equipment, visit the **Musée Flaubert** (51 rue de Lecat; Tue 10am–12.30pm 2–6pm, Wed–Sat 2–6pm).

Jumièges

The D982 leading west from Rouen is the start of the **Route des Abbayes**, which meanders through woodland and meadows around the medieval Norman abbeys – most of them enjoying their golden period under William the Conqueror – at St-Martin-de-Boscherville, Jumièges, St-Wandrille, Le Bec-Hellouin and Caen, culminating in the masterpiece, Mont-St-Michel.

The delightful little harbour of Honfleur

Early morning on the beach at Deauville

The ruins of the huge **abbey** of **Jumièges** ㉓ are perhaps the most impressive: the white-granite shells of two churches, the Romanesque Notre-Dame and the smaller Gothic St-Pierre. Duke William returned from his conquest of England to attend the consecration of Notre-Dame in 1067. Seven centuries later, the Benedictine monastery was disbanded by the Revolution. The sturdy edifices resisted total destruction and are still dominated by Notre-Dame's two soaring square towers, minus their original spires.

Honfleur

Situated on the Seine estuary, the pretty port of **Honfleur** ㉔ has witnessed the beginning of many seafaring adventures – including Samuel de Champlain's departure for what would become Quebec – and is still a Mecca for sailors. Artists are also fond of this harbour and its constantly changing light; among 19th-century visitors were Cézanne, Corot, Monet, Seurat and Sisley. Painters still flock to Honfleur today.

Towering over the sheltered yachting harbour of the **Vieux Bassin** are tall houses with slate and timber facades. The old shipbuilders' quarter, along **rue Haute**, is well worth exploring. It runs westward from the Lieutenance, the 16th-century remains of the royal governor's house at the mouth of the harbour. Among the several museums in Honfleur are the **Musée de la Marine** (Apr–Sept Tue–Sun 10am–noon, 2–6.30pm, shorter hours Oct–Mar), with a collection of nautical treasures, housed in the 14th-century Eglise St-Etienne (quai St-Etienne); and the **Musée Eugène Boudin** (place Erik Satie; daily Wed–Mon 10am–noon, Apr–Jun and Sep 2–6pm, Oct–Mar 2.30–5.30pm), with a rich display of paintings.

The **Pont de Normandie**, only 2km (1 mile) from Honfleur, is an elegant bridge spanning the mouth of the Seine, and giving access to the port of Le Havre. Completed in 1995, it shattered the previous record for cable-stayed bridges, with a span of 856m (2,808ft).

Deauville

Blending old-fashioned elegance with modern comforts, the most prosperous of Normandy's seaside resorts is also the most expensive. But even if your budget doesn't extend to staying in **Deauville**, take a walk along its wooden promenade *(planches)* and participate in one of the town's favourite activities: people-watching. The town attracts celebrities and fashion models who come here to have their photographs taken on the boardwalk.

Horse-lovers come for the summer racing – flat and steeple – and for the prestigious yearling sale in August. What they win on the racing, they gamble at the casino. The

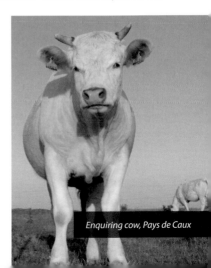

Enquiring cow, Pays de Caux

tennis and golf are first class. Yachtsmen should bear in mind a rather gloomy Deauville proverb: if you can see the port of Le Havre, it will rain in the afternoon, and if you can't, it's already raining.

Côte Fleurie

Between the estuaries of the Touques and Dives rivers, 20km (12 miles) of sandy beaches, handsome villas and weather-beaten old hotels give a nostalgic peek at Napoleon III's Second Empire and the Belle Epoque of the 1900s.

The oldest of this coast's resorts, **Trouville**, now seems rather like a slightly down-market version of Deauville, albeit one that is just as lively. It has a pretty harbour and the bistros on the quayside serve excellent seafood.

The charm of **Houlgate** lies in the trees and flowers of its gardens and its sandy beach. Take the long walk at low tide east to the rocks known as the **Vaches Noires** (Black Cows), because they resemble a herd of cattle tumbling into the sea.

Cabourg is the most stately of the old Channel resorts. Marcel Proust spent many summers at its splendid **Grand Hôtel**, where he wrote part of his *A la Recherche du Temps Perdu*.

Pays d'Auge

Inland from the Côte Fleurie, the countryside reflects the popular image of Normandy: orchards, rolling valleys and massive timbered manor houses; the land where apples are turned into cider and Calvados and dairies churn out pungent, creamy Camembert, Livarot and Pont-l'Evêque.

The well-marked **Route du Cidre** and **Route du Fromage** are good guides to the towns and villages of the area, including the picturesque village of **Beuvron en Auge**. Local tourist offices (see page 247) will direct you to farms where you can sample and buy regional cheeses – more fun than in the unexceptional towns of Camembert, Livarot and Pont-l'Evêque themselves. Drivers should be wary of the strong cider.

Caen

The powerful and purposeful town of **Caen** ㉓ is a bustling, business-like centre of commerce, forever arranging trade fairs and exhibitions, and its lively university makes for a vivacious nightlife and cultural scene, too. Little remains of Caen's historic centre, but its good hotels and excellent seafood restaurants make it, with Bayeux, a useful starting-point for visits to the Normandy invasion beaches. Caen was a major objective of the Allies in the 1944 landings. It took two months to capture and was devastated by Allied bombs and the shells of the retreating Germans.

Fortunately, the noble silhouette of the **Abbaye aux Hommes** has survived (best seen from the place Louis-Guillouard). Its church, the **Eglise St-Etienne** (both daily but times can vary; tours of Abbey available), harmoniously combines its Romanesque towers and nave with Gothic steeples, choir and chancel. It was begun in the momentous year of 1066, and William the Conqueror made its first abbot his archbishop

The Bayeux Tapestry

Bagnoles-de-l'Orne

Normandy's Bagnoles-de-l'Orne is one of France's iconic spa towns, filled with large institutions and residences for those with rheumatic disorders. It is worth a visit as it represents a communal and holistic approach to health many Westerners would find surprising.

of Canterbury. The elegant 18th-century monastery buildings are now Caen's town hall.

The remains of William's 11th-century **château** house the **Musée des Beaux-Arts** (mba.caen.fr; Apr–late Sept Mon–Fri 9.30am–12.30pm, 2–6pm, Sat–Sun 11am–6pm, late Sept–Mar Wed–Sun 9.30am–12.30pm, 2–6pm) and an excellent collection of European painting. Highlights include Poussin's *Mort d'Adonis*, Veronese's *Tentation de St Antoine*, Rubens' *Abraham et Melchisédech* and Boudin's *La Plage de Deauville*. The nearby **Musée de Normandie** (musee-de-normandie.caen.fr; Mon–Fri 9.30am–12.30pm, 2–6pm, Sat–Sun 11am–6pm, closed Mon–Tue late Sept–mid-Apr) makes a handsome introduction the region, with displays on its history, archaeology and ethnography.

Le Mémorial – Un Musée pour la Paix (Museum for Peace, esplanade General Eisenhower) is a modern interactive exhibition, placing the events of D-Day and World War II in the context of the 20th century as a whole.

Bayeux

The first French town to be liberated in World War II (on the day after D-Day), **Bayeux** ㉖ was blessedly preserved from destruction. Its Gothic cathedral dominates a pretty **old town** *(vieille ville)* of medieval and Renaissance houses.

But the town's most cherished treasure is the magnificent **Bayeux Tapestry** (or more accurately, embroidery), which was created for the consecration of Bayeux Cathedral in 1077 to tell the story of Duke William's conquest of England. It is lovingly mounted in the Grand

Seminary of the **Centre Guillaume-le-Conquérant** (www.bayeux museum.com; Mar–Oct 9am–6.30pm, May–Aug until 7pm, Feb and Nov–Dec 9.30am–12.30pm, 2–6pm, closed Jan), in rue de Nesmond, and is accompanied by a fascinating film (in English or French) explaining the work's historical background. Audio commentary headsets are available to bring the pictures to life.

The Bayeux Tapestry tells the story of the invasion of England from the Norman point of view, showing the English King Harold as a treacherous weakling who cheated the noble William of Normandy out of the throne promised him by King Edward the Confessor. No dreary piece of obscure medieval decoration, the beautifully coloured 70m (230ft) tapestry gives a vivid and often humorous picture of life at William's court, with insights into medieval cooking, lovemaking and preparations for war. These and the climactic Battle of Hastings are depicted with all the exciting action and violence of a modern adventure film, played out by a cast of 626 characters, 202 horses, 55 dogs and 505 other animals.

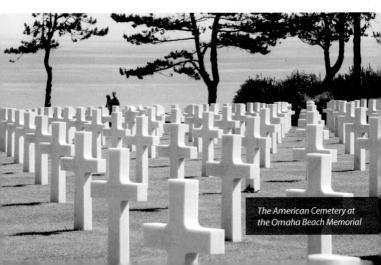

The American Cemetery at the Omaha Beach Memorial

Omaha and Utah

The Americans' Omaha and Utah beaches, from Colleville to La Madeleine, are official map references, a cartographer's tribute to the theatre of the fiercest fighting in the D-Day landings. The desolate coastline recalls the stormy conditions that prevented the Americans from setting up an artificial harbour to land their equipment. The 9,386 white marble crosses of the American military cemetery overlook Omaha Beach.

D-Day Beaches

Before 6 June 1944 the peaceful stretch of coast west of Cabourg, from Ouistreham to the Cotentin peninsula, was known simply as the Côte du Calvados, a flat, undramatic shoreline broken by a few unspectacular chalk cliffs and sand dunes. And then, at 6.30am on D-Day, came the first of a fleet of 4,266 vessels to turn the beaches into beachheads (known as the **D-Day landing beaches** ㉗) with their now famous code names: **Sword**, **Juno**, **Gold**, **Omaha**, and **Utah**.

Today the visitor will find an atmosphere of rather bleak serenity that is in itself as evocative as the remaining concrete bunkers and simple monuments on the sites of the action and the miles of crosses in the military cemeteries. There are also many excellent museums commemorating the battles. For more information, visit www.normandie44lamemoire.com.

To see where the British and Canadians, with the support of the Free French forces, attacked on the eastern half of the beaches, start out at the port town of **Ouistreham/Riva-Bella** and drive west along the coast road to **Bernières** and **Courseulles** (where the Canadians staged their **Juno Beach** landings, marked by monuments on the beaches) and then the Canadians' cemetery 4km (2.5 miles) to the south at Reviers.

At **Arromanches** you can see the most fascinating monument to British ingenuity in the Allied landings – the remains of a **Mulberry harbour**. The floating steel-and-concrete jetties and pontoons, hauled across the English Channel, were the only way of unloading tanks and heavy artillery on the **gold beach** coastline without natural harbours. The **Musée du Débarquement** (tel: 02 31 22 34 31; www.musee-arromanches.fr; daily mid Mar–Dec, variable hours) includes a film detailing one of the momentous days in history of the modern era.

The **Musée du Débarquement Utah** (www.utah-beach.com; daily June–Sept 9.30am–7pm, Oct–May 10am–6pm, Nov 10am–5pm) and monument are 5km (3 miles) inland from La Madeleine, near Ste-Marie-du-Mont. Staff at the local tourist offices will be able to direct you to other museums and to the region's 27 Allied and German military cemeteries.

Mont-St-Michel

The island sanctuary of **Mont-St-Michel** 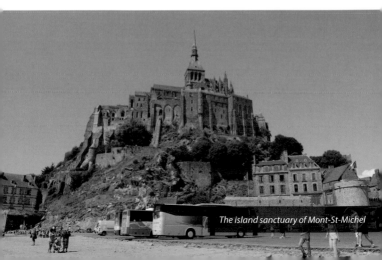 at the border between Normandy and Brittany is a wonder of the Western world. That first glimpse of the towering, steepled abbey (www.ot-montsaintmichel.com; daily May–Aug 9am–7pm, Sept–Apr 9.30am–6pm) rising from the sea on its rock is a moment you will not forget. If you're coming

The island sanctuary of Mont-St-Michel

from Caen, stop in Avranches for a panorama of the bay from the Jardin des Plantes, or drive out to the coast road (D911) between St-Jean-Le-Thomas and Carolles. From other directions, head for the coast road via Courtils for that all-important vista. Unfortunately, the crowds of tourists in the summer can be overwhelming, and some visitors prefer to admire Mont-St-Michel from a distance. The view of the illuminated mount at night is spectacular from the other side of the bay at le Grouin du Sud.

The bay around the island's granite outcrop has steadily silted up in recent years, so that it's isolated only during very high tides. These are most dramatic during the spring and autumn equinox, when the sea comes in at nearly 50m (164ft) a minute over a distance of 15km (9 miles). This proved dangerous to pilgrims who approached the abbey across the sands (the causeway joining the island to the mainland was not built until 1874). No cars can park at the base of the *mont*, instead park in one of several large car parks and take a shuttle bus or walk.

In the 8th century, on what was once a Celtic burial ground (originally called Mont-Tombe), the bishop of the nearby town of Avranches began by building an oratory – at the prompting, he claimed, of the Archangel Michael. In 1017 Benedictine monks started work on the flat-roofed abbey shown in the Bayeux Tapestry.

BATTLING THROUGH BOCAGE

Memoirs of the Normandy fighting are haunted by the word *bocage* – small fields enclosed by hedgerows. Grown since Celtic times, the hedgerows had so stiffened the banks with their roots that the Americans had to improvise special bulldozers to cut through them. Troops moving through *bocage* confronted at intervals of 90m (100yds) a succession of perfect defensive positions for snipers and machine-gunners. The roadways between the hedgerows had worn so deep below the level of the surrounding fields that they could even conceal a tank.

La Mère Poulard is a Mont-St-Michel institution

By the 14th century, the abbey was surrounded by a fortified village. The pilgrims flocked here throughout the Hundred Years' War, paying tolls to the English, who controlled the surrounding territory – though they never succeeded in breaking through the mount's defences. After a period of steady decline, the monastery was dismantled even before the Revolution. It was saved from total destruction only to end up, ignominiously, as a state prison. Today, however, the *mont* is once again flooded with pilgrims and is a truly awe-inspiring experience.

If you make your way to the upper terrace of the *mont*, which commands splendid views of the bay, a variety of guided tours (conducted in English, French or German) will take you down through three levels of abbey buildings: the church, cloister and refectory at the top; the Salle des Chevaliers (Knights' Hall) and Salle des Hôtes (Guests' Hall) in the middle; and the storeroom and almonry underneath.

The **abbey church** combines a sturdy Romanesque nave with a more airy Flamboyant Gothic chancel. The choir and chancel do not stand on the island's granite core but on a platform formed by three crypts, with the massive columns of the **Crypte des Gros Piliers** doing most of the work.

In a magical space overlooking the sea, the beautifully sculpted columns of the cloister create a perfect framework of grace and delicacy for a moment's meditation. With the cloister, the monks' ethereally lit refectory, the grand Knights' Hall and the elegant **Guests' Hall** together make up the masterpiece of Gothic architecture that earned the abbey the name **La Merveille** ('Wonder').

BRITTANY

The province of Brittany, as its residents will tell you, is a country apart, proud of its regional culture and guarding its seclusion from the rest of France. The sea beckons many visitors to Brittany, with a combination of a craggy coastline and great sandy beaches, seaside resorts on the Côte d'Emeraude (Emerald Coast) and small harbour towns on the Golfe du Morbihan. But much fun can be had hiking in the forests and rocky landscapes between Huelgoat and Roc Trévezel and exploring the prehistoric *menhir* country around Carnac and the Parish Closes (*enclos paroissiaux*).

Côte d'Emeraude

The Emerald Coast's 70km (43 miles) of rugged cliffs and caves alternate with quiet resorts offering sandy beaches. The little port town of **Cancale** – with a wide vista across the bay of Mont-St-Michel – has been a major centre of oyster-breeding since earliest Celtic times. You can examine the oyster beds from the port's jetty, the **Jetée de la Fenêtre**.

The coast road takes you west to **Pointe du Grouin**, a cliff 40m (130ft) high, with a spectacular view of the Chausey Islands to the north and to **St-Malo** ㉙, a town steeped in seafaring history; its sailors left their name as far afield as the Malouines, claimed by the British as the Falkland Islands. St-Malo remains a busy fishing port, ferry terminal and yacht harbour.

St-Malo suffered severe bomb damage during World War II, but the old town, surrounded on three sides by the sea, has been tastefully restored. Its ramparts, built and rebuilt from the 12th to 18th centuries,

The Cap Fréhel, a rewarding landscape for ramblers

make for a bracing walk, with the stretch between the St-Philippe bastion and the Tour Bidouane opening up a vista along the whole Emerald Coast. At low tide you can risk a quick walk or wade out to the little island of Grand Bé, with its simple, unadorned tomb of the locally born Romantic writer Chateaubriand.

A 7.5 km walking loop (www.saint-malo-tourisme.co.uk) passes through La Passagère, the neighboring village, which still houses the ferryman's house. Here, you'll find a graveyard of old boats; look out for L'Endormie, which has a fresco by local painter Kalvez on its hull.

Like many French seaside resorts, **Dinard** was a 'discovery' of the British in the 19th century, who called it 'Queen of the Emerald Coast'. The British, followed by Americans, appreciated the broad, sheltered beach and the particularly mild microclimate – palms, fig trees, tamarisk and camellias all flourish here.

In a still faintly Victorian atmosphere, Dinard has preserved the Gothic mansions that well-to-do merchants built here in the early 1900s, while transforming itself into a modern resort, in contrast with the cosily rustic atmosphere of St-Malo.

Grabbing a bargain at the flea market

The pink sandstone cliffs at **Cap Fréhel**, 70m (230ft) above the sea, look out across the Grande and Petite Fauconnière bird sanctuaries, with their colonies of cormorants and guillemots.

Dinan

Inland from the Côte d'Emeraude, on the Rance river, is the pretty market town of **Dinan** ㉚. The ramparts of its old town *(vieille ville)* enclose medieval cobbled streets and half-timbered houses. Climb the 15th-century clock tower in rue de l'Horloge or visit Le Jardin Anglais, in front of the 12th-century Basilique St-Saveur, for a good view over the river, port and viaduct.

The Parish Close Road

The *enclos paroissial* (parish close) epitomises the religious life in rural Brittany during the 16th to 18th centuries. These architectural ensembles encompass church, cemetery, charnel house (or ossuary) and calvary (a unique free standing structure with carvings illustrating Bible scenes, often with characters in contemporary dress), all grouped in a square and entered via a triumphal arch. The elaborate interiors and decorations are attributed to rivalry between neighbouring villages.

In a morning's tour from Morlaix, about 160km (100 miles) west of Dinard, you can take in three of the most important parish closes on a route signposted: *Circuit des Enclos Paroissiaux.*

St-Thégonnec is an outstanding example, its triumphal arch setting the tone for the majestic **calvary** of 1610. The **ossuary**, now a chapel, is late Renaissance in the very elaborate Breton manner – with Corinthian columns, lanterns, niches and caryatids. The **church** has an even more elaborate Baroque pulpit.

More than 200 Old and New Testament figures are sculpted on the **calvary** at **Guimiliau**. The **church** has granite statues of Jesus and the Apostles adorning its porch. Although a lightning bolt toppled the tower of the **church of Lampaul-Guimiliau** in 1809, the church's interior remains impressive. The 16th-century polychrome rood beam spanning the nave is decorated with scenes from the Passion.

Huelgoat

The pretty little town of **Huelgoat** is mainly attractive as a base for excursions into the nature reserve of forests, rivers and pools in the **Parc Régional d'Armorique**. You can fish for perch and carp in the lake or for trout in the *Rivière d'Argent* (Silver River). At the top end of the lake, you wander into dense forest through a fantastic chaos of rocks and grottos.

Brest

With an important sheltered harbour at the western tip of Brittany, **Brest ㉛** is a lively university city. The city has the sea in its bones, celebrated at the **Musée National de la Marine** (www.musee-marine.fr; Apr–Sept daily 10am–6.30pm, Oct–Mar Wed–Mon 1.30–6.30pm,

The Breton tongue

Breton is the only Celtic language spoken on the European continent, but the language has no official status and only around 250,000 people are fluent speakers.

closed Jan), which is located in an imposing chateau and displays a superlative collection of ship models. With plenty of restaurants and a vibrant nightlife, plus bracing walks and cultural venues, Brest has much to offer.

Carnac

Like the wild countryside of the interior, the megalithic monuments of Brittany's **menhir country** on the south coast take you back into the legends and mists of time.

Carnac ㉜ is surrounded by fields with thousands of gigantic stones *(menhirs)* arranged in mysterious alignments and patterns set up over centuries beginning as early as 5500BC. Scholars have suggested the alignments are associated with cults of the sun or moon, or are astronomical arrangements for predicting such phenomena as eclipses.

The alignments occupy three main fields a short walk north of the town. **Le Ménec**, the biggest, has 1,099 *menhirs* in 12 rows (plus 70 *menhirs* in a circle or *cromlech* around part of the hamlet of Le Ménec). The

Menhirs at Carnac

field of **Kermario** has a dolmen (chamber built of flat slabs on pillars) and 1,029 *menhirs* in 10 rows. Among them is the Giant of Manio, a *menhir* over 6m (20ft) high, shaped like a clenched fist. Most impressive is the **Kerlescan** alignment, 594 *menhirs* that form what locals call the frozen army. The best time to see them all is early morning, looming out of the mist, or at sunset, throwing dramatic shadows. The **Musée de la Préhistoire** (www.museedecarnac.com; 10 place de la Chapelle; Apr–June and Sept 10am–12.30pm, 2–6pm,

The Loire at Saumur

July–Aug 10am–6.30pm, Oct 10am–12.30pm, 2–5.30pm, Nov and Mar, Wed–Mon 2–5.30pm) exhibits artefacts representative of local life during the Paleolithic, Neolithic, Bronze, Iron and Roman ages.

La Baule

South of Carnac is the 5-km (3-mile) beach of **La Baule,** one of France's most perfectly formed Atlantic beaches. Although swallowed up by the region of Pays de la Loire, formed in 1955, the resort very much retains its Breton roots. An elegant ribbon of fine sand stretches from Pornichet to Le Pouliguen in a perfect half-moon, past upmarket sailing and beach clubs and along an esplanade of luxury hotels with a casino right at the centre.

If you tire of the easy life on the beachfront, take a trip west to the wilder coast of the peninsula past Batz-sur-Mer (pronounced *Bah*) to the pretty little fishing port and resort of Le Croisic.

LOIRE VALLEY

The Loire is the longest river in France – flowing an impressive 1,010km (630 miles) from its source in the Vivarais mountains south of St-Etienne to its estuary west of Nantes – but the region, home to some of the most spectacular châteaux in France, covers barely a fifth of that distance. The counts and courtiers came here for the lush, fertile valleys and to be close to the French royalty who held court and hunted here for centuries.

The route we propose for visitors driving from Paris on the *autoroute,* exits at Orléans and then on to Blois and, after a side trip to Chambord, heads west on the D952 to Angers. Unless in a hurry take the non-toll road, the D723, which parallels the Loire, and head for Nantes. Simply reverse the route if you're coming from Brittany.

For centuries, the Loire was a vital highway between the Atlantic and the heart of France. Commercial traffic declined during the 17th and 18th centuries but was revived with the advent of the steamship in 1832; the river then suffered due to silting and the onslaught of the railways. Today, the Loire is a sleepy waterway, running deep only with heavy rains or spring thaws.

Orléans

The historic city of **Orléans** ㉝ on the Loire has always been strategic, located at the river's most northerly point and thus the closest point to Paris. Famed for the legendary Joan of Arc, who was burned at the stake in 1431 during the Hundred Years' War with the English; her life is celebrated in a lively festival each May. Bombed in World War Two it was one of the first cities to be rebuilt after liberation. With its fine **cathedral**, excellent **museums** and attractive streets, and just one hour from Paris, it makes a good base for visiting the châteaux of the Loire Valley.

Blois

Situated on a hill overlooking the Loire, **Blois** ㉞ invites the visitor to linger in the narrow winding streets that lead from the cathedral to the château, pausing to admire the handsome old houses on the place St-Louis and rue Porte-Chartraine.

The royal **château** (www.chateaudeblois.fr; daily July–Aug 9am– 7pm, Apr–June and Sept–Oct 9am–6.30pm, Nov–Mar 10am–5pm) is fascinating for its variety of styles from the 13th to 17th centuries. The entrance to the château is through the brick-and-stone gateway of the late Gothic Louis XII wing, completed in 1503. Across the courtyard on the right-hand side is the château's splendid François I wing. It was built only a decade after the Louis XII wing but, reflecting the contrast between the debonair Renaissance prince and his dour predecessor, is a world apart in elegance and panache.

Of particular interest on the first floor of the François I wing is the wood-panelled cabinet (study) of Catherine de Médicis, conniving queen mother and regent to three kings of France. Many of the 237 carved panels, each different, were believed to conceal poisons, as well as jewels and state papers. On the second floor, in 1588, her son Henri III used not poison but a dozen men armed with swords and daggers to do away with his arch rival, Duke Henri de Guise.

Chambord

Upriver, east of Blois, in a huge and densely wooded park surrounded by 31km (19 miles) of high walls, the brilliant white **Château de Chambord** (www. chambord.org; daily Nov–Mar 9am–5pm, Apr–Oct 9am–6pm) is the most extravagant of all the royal residences in the Loire Valley. To have easy access to the wild boar and deer (which can still be seen from observation platforms in the park), François I built himself this glorified 440-room hunting lodge. Construction began in 1519 and was largely finished by 1547.

Renaissance ladder, Blois

Ignominious death

Some kings die for their country, others for beliefs. Unfortunately, on the eve of Palm Sunday 1498, Charles VIII hit his head on a door in Amboise while trying to get to a lavatory. He died nine hours later where he fell, no-one having dared to move him.

Apart from its sheer size, Chambord is arguably most famous for its striking roofline – a surprisingly harmonious blend of cupolas, domes, turrets, spires and chimneys, all of which have led to it being described as 'the skyline of Constantinople on a single building'. It is believed that Leonardo da Vinci, whom François brought to the Loire Valley in 1516, participated in the design, especially of the central four-towered *donjon* – which makes a dream palace out of a classically feudal castle keep – and the celebrated double-ramped spiral staircase in the donjon's centre, which enables people to go up and down without meeting. The interior itself is sparsely furnished.

Amboise

From Blois, follow the D952 along the right bank of the Loire before crossing over to **Amboise** for a view of the exterior of the château that housed many of France's kings. Although a large part of the château complex no longer stands, it remains impressive. An unusual feature is the huge spiral ramp of the Tour des Minimes, wide enough to allow access for horses and provisions. Some of the interior has been refurbished in recent years, and there is a good collection of furniture. The château became a possession of the French throne in 1434, and Leonardo da Vinci spent his last days in a small manor house nearby, the Clos-Lucé, now a museum illustrating his talents. A bust in the château gardens marks his grave.

Chenonceau

One of the most elegant Renaissance châteaux, **Chenonceau** is noted for its long gallery raised on arches to span the Cher river. The château (www.

chenonceau.com; daily July–Aug 9am–7pm, Sept until 7.30pm, June until 6pm, shorter hours rest of year) was owned by a series of women including Diane de Poitiers, mistress to Henri II, and Catherine de Médicis.

In the apartments, in addition to 16th-century tapestries and fine furniture, you'll see Diane's neatly kept household accounts. No-one knows whether Primaticcio's contemporary portrait of her as Diana, the goddess of hunting, does full justice to her beauty.

After Henri's death, his widow, Catherine de Médicis, took Chenonceau for herself and added the galleried floors of ballrooms and reception halls completing the bridge across the river. Tours of the château are self-guided, and there are impressive formal gardens and a large park. Boat rides are available on the river when the water is deep enough.

Loches

To the south of the town of Chenonceaux, on the Indre river, the medieval village of Loches is as much an attraction as the château itself. The

The elegant Château de Chenonceau

The streets of Angers

Collegiate Church of St-Ours (daily July–Aug 9am–10pm, shorter hours for the rest of the year; free) is a superb piece of Romanesque architecture.

Stroll along rue St-Ours and the rue du Château, then wander around the ramparts. Particularly interesting is the 11th-century keep and dungeon, which formed part of the town's defences. Two 15th-century additions served as prisons for royal enemies.

At the other end of the fortifications, the terrace of the **Logis Royal** (Royal Lodge) affords a delightful view over the village and the Indre Valley. Architecturally, the lodge offers a striking transition from sober Gothic to more decorative Renaissance. A notable feature is Anne de Bretagne's private oratory, built *c.*1500 and a masterpiece of the Flamboyant Gothic style.

Azay-le-Rideau

Just to the southwest of Tours, with walls of dazzling white stone under grey slate roofs, **Azay-le-Rideau**'s château (www.azay-le-rideau.fr; daily July–Aug 9.30am–7pm, Sept and Apr–June 9.30am–6pm, Oct–Mar 10am–5.15pm) forms a beautiful reflection in the waters of the Indre river, 30km (19 miles) southwest of Tours.

It was erected in the early 16th century by François I's corrupt treasurer, Gilles Berthelot, part of it on a Venetian-style foundation of timber piles driven into the bed of the river. Berthelot's wife supervised the design, and the delicacy of its forms.

Madame Berthelot had the large vaulted kitchen built almost on a level with the river, so that an indoor well provided the closest thing to running water, and an unusually hygienic stone drain sent back the slops. You can see the kind of utensils and cake tins her cooks would have used – at least, until the château was confiscated by the king for Berthelot's misdeeds. There are special shows for families on summer evenings.

Saumur

Heading west from Azay-le-Rideau towards Angers, you can't miss the towering **Château de Saumur** (www.chateau-saumur.fr; Tue–Sun, Oct–Mar 10am–1pm 2–5.30pm, Apr–Jun and Sept 10am–6pm, July–Aug 10am–7pm, closed Jan). The town of **Saumur** ③ is also known for its sparkling wine and for the caves where approximately 70 percent of France's cultivated mushrooms are grown. In fact, the Saumur region is the world's leading mushroom producer, and a single cave can produce up to 12 tons in one day. The fascinating **Musée du Champignon** (www.musee-du-champignon.com; rues St-Hilaire and St-Florent; daily Apr–Sep 10am–7pm, Oct–Mar until 6pm, closed Dec and Jan) explains the whole process and displays fossils found in the caves as well as a troglodyte family's home. These cave-dwellers dug into the soft porous rock around the cliffs and shore of the Loire, made up of layers of shells from the river, to make their idiosyncratic shelters and caves from early Christian times onwards. Many are still occupied; some are used as wine cellars and mushroom farms.

Angers

Angers ③ , the ancient capital of Anjou, is considered to be one of the most beautiful cities in France and is home to many museums and buildings of interest, including the imposing 12th- and 13th-century Gothic Cathédrale St-Maurice. If not the most beautiful, the **château** (www.

chateau-angers.fr; daily May–Aug 10am–6.30pm, Sept–Apr 10am–5.30pm) is certainly the most formidable in the Loire Valley, a real defensive fortress, its black ramparts still forbidding despite having had their towers decapitated on the orders of Henri III. The château's proudest possession is the great 14th-century Apocalypse Tapestry narrating the gospel of St John in detail. The 75 wonderfully detailed panels reveal John observing and reacting to his fantastic visions.

The beautifully restored ruins of the 13th-century Eglise Toussaint have been incorporated into the **Galerie David d'Angers** (musees.angers.fr; 33 rue Toussaint; Tue–Sun 10am–6pm), which houses a unique collection of the sculptor's portrayals of notables including Honoré de Balzac, Victor Hugo, Gutenberg, Paganini and George Washington.

Nantes

Although located on the Loire, culturally and historically **Nantes** 37 is a Breton city and many locals campaign to return it to Brittany. Its history can be followed at the Château des Ducs de Bretagne in the **Musée d'Histoire de Nantes** (www.chateaunantes.fr; July–Aug daily 10am–7pm, rest of year Tue–Sun 10am–6pm). The city is popular with young professionals as an alternative to Paris, and as a result it has a vibrant nightlife and plenty of cultural venues. Highlights also include Les Machines de l'Ile, an artistic project that combines the imaginary worlds of Jules Verne, the mechanical ambitions of Da Vinci and Nantes' industrial past. All this culminates in huge mechanical constructions that move and work in astonishing ways; the most famous is the enormous elephant which stalks the banks of the Loire, squirting water from its trunk, but a gigantic heron tree sunk in a nearby quarry is due for launch in 2023.

THE SOUTHEAST

The southeast of France, from the Alps down through the Rhône Valley to Provence and the Côte d'Azur (also known as the French Riviera), is France's, and indeed the world's, playground, with resorts catering to tourists' needs in both summer and winter. Whether you prefer lying on a beach, leisurely strolls, off-piste skiing or summer mountain hikes, you will find what you want here.

The outdoor life in the Savoie Alps and the resorts around Mont Blanc can be as exhilarating in summer as in winter. Though less energetic, life is equally refreshing down on the lovely lakes of Annecy and Le Bourget. The Rhône Valley region around Lyon is the epicentre of French gastronomy, while further south, in Provence, the climate and the slow Mediterranean lifestyle take charge. There are Roman ruins and feudal fortresses to explore, but you can also do some serious lounging under shady trees and in pavement cafés. We also suggest a small selection of holiday resorts and excursions on Napoleon's wild and beautiful island of Corsica.

SAVOIE

The once-remote province of Savoie, long an independent duchy, voted to become a part of France in 1860. The French had little interest in the

Yachts in St-Tropez

Alps until the mountain-climbing craze was launched by the conquest of Mont Blanc in 1786.

However, the high mountains, lakes and spas of Savoie are not just for climbers and skiiers. Vast fields of wildflowers welcome the spring visitor, and in summer horse-riding, mountain biking, tennis, rafting, hang-gliding and paragliding now join the more traditional activities of climbing and hiking.

Even in summer, you should keep a sweater and sunglasses with you for sudden changes in temperature and for the brilliant sunlight, and bear in mind the rarefied atmosphere when exercising.

Chamonix

It wasn't until 1924, with the first Winter Olympic Games at **Chamonix** ❸⓿, that skiing – at the time only cross-country – attracted international attention. Today the slopes are packed in winter and although the newer resorts lack the charm of the traditional villages, the scenery remains unbeatable. The neighbourhood around the town's main church has enough old-fashioned charm to retain something of the town's 19th-century pioneering atmosphere. For a fuller sense of how it felt to come here when mountain-climbing and skiing were in their infancy, spend an hour or so in the **Musée Alpin** (www.musee-alpin-chamonix.fr; temporarily closed for renovation), tracing the history of the region, its heroes and their remarkable pioneering exploits, in photos and displays of equipment.

The cable-car *(téléphérique)* ride up to the **Aiguille du Midi** (literally meaning 'middle needle') is the most spectacular in the French Alps, offering

Lac d'Annecy

The entire 38-km (24-mile) circuit of Lac d'Annecy can be driven, walked or cycled around and is famed for its beauty. There's even a marathon every April. Among others, Cézanne gave his post-Impressionist spin on the lake's tumbling headlands and earthy shorelines.

The 12th-century Palais de L'Isle in Annecy

a breathtaking view of **Mont Blanc**'s snow-covered peak (altitude: 4,808m/15,770ft) and the surrounding landscape. For some easy hiking, stop off at the lower station of Plan de l'Aiguille (2,310m/7,580ft). The cable car up to **Le Brévent** (2,525m/8,284ft), northwest of Chamonix, will give you a panoramic view of the whole north face of Mont Blanc and the Aiguille du Midi. For a close-up view of a glacier and formidable ice caves, take the cable car and rack railway up the Montenvers to the dazzling **Mer de Glace** (Sea of Ice).

Annecy

The lovely old town of **Annecy** ㊳, complete with swans, a pristine Alpine lake and a backdrop of snowcapped mountains, is picture perfect. Strolling along the waterfront promenades and through the narrow streets, and taking boat trips on the lake are the main attractions in summer. The town is associated with the philosopher Jean-Jacques Rousseau, who met Madame de Warrens here after his flight from Geneva.

One of the major sights in the town is the much-photographed, triangular-shaped, 12th-century **Palais de l'Isle**, which stands in the middle

Hautecombe Abbey

of the Thiou river like the prow of a boat. The building has filled numerous roles over the years, from residence to jail to mint, and is now employed for exhibitions.

The magnificent **Château d'Annecy** (musees.annecy. fr; Wed–Mon, June–Sept 10.30am–6pm, Oct–May 10am–noon, 2–5pm), former home of the Counts of Geneva, contains an interesting museum devoted to local archaeology and folklore and the natural history of the Alps. The château's terrace is the best spot for pictures of the old town.

Cruises around the **Lac d'Annecy** start from the Thiou river. Some of them include a cable-car ride to the top of **Mont Veyrier** (1,291m/ 4,235ft) and its spectacular panorama of the Alps, but all will give you a wonderful view of the jagged snowcapped peaks of the Dents de Lanfon and the rugged La Tournette to the east, as well as the gentler Entrevernes and Taillefer mountains to the west.

As a detour, take the D909 east to the Mont Veyrier cable car, continuing on to the pretty town of **Menthon-St-Bernard** and its medieval castle high above the lake. The D42 takes you up to the **Col de la Forclaz** (1,157m/3,796ft).

Aix-les-Bains

This elegant spa town of **Aix-les-Bains** ⑩, on the edge of the Lac du Bourget, has offered cures for rheumatism and other ailments for centuries. The 4th-century Roman emperor Gratianus was an early visitor, followed by such luminaries as the poet Alphonse de Lamartine, Queen Victoria and composers Saint-Saëns and Rachmaninov.

In recent years the French national health system has approved reimbursement for spa treatments and the number of *curistes* seeking treatment has risen. Some 30,000 people attend the spas each year. There are lots of spas in Aix, one of the biggest is **Station Thermale Nationaux** (www.valvital.fr). Swimming, waterskiing, windsurfing and sailing are all available on the lake, as are boat cruises. One popular cruise destination (leaving from the Grand Port) is to the neo-Gothic **Abbaye de Hautecombe**.

The town's **Musée Faure** (www.aixlesbains.fr/; boulevard des Côtes; Wed–Sun 10am–12.30pm, 2–6pm) contains a number of Rodin bronzes and watercolours, and works by Degas, Pissarro, Corot and Cézanne.

THE RHÔNE VALLEY

From its source high in the Swiss Alps, the Rhône flows almost due south to the Mediterranean. The Rhône Valley has always been a central artery; a channel for river, road and rail traffic between the north and south. It was the route of the Romans' invasion of Gaul, and the key to Lyon's wealth in the Middle Ages.

The farmers of the Lyon region benefit from a subtle mixture of the cooler and damper north with the first hints of Mediterranean warmth and light. Some of the best food in the country is produced here: poultry from Bresse; freshwater fish from the Savoie lakes; Charolais beef; pears, apples and cherries from orchards to the north of town; and peaches and apricots from the ones to the south.

The fruit industry started in earnest in the 1880s as a reaction to the phylloxera disease that struck the local vineyards.

Wine by the litre

Some of the Lyon winery cooperatives produce very good wines. However, much of it doesn't travel well and is therefore never exported. In many cases you can take empty containers to cooperatives, and they will fill them with wine for a very reasonable price.

Today, the **Beaujolais country** thrives and wine-lovers heading south detour to familiar names such as Fleurie, Juliénas, Chénas, Morgon and Brouilly. Further south, opposite Tournon, there is the lure of the celebrated *Côtes du Rhône* at Tain-l'Hermitage.

Lyon

Located at the crossroads between north and south, **Lyon** ❹ was the ideal choice as the Roman capital of Gaul. The silk trade played a large role in Lyon's expansion in the 16th century, and France's second-largest city remains a prosperous and growing banking, textile and industrial centre with an important cultural heritage and a lively arts scene; all just two hours from Paris by TGV.

Food is an important part of any visit to Lyon – legendary chef Paul Bocuse was based here until his death in 2018. In addition to the great shrines of *haute cuisine* in and around the city, you should seek out the little bars and cafés and the old-fashioned bistros that the Lyonnais call

A typical bouchon lyonnais

bouchons (after the bunches of straw they used as bottle-stoppers and which served as signs for their restaurants).

Lyon is not an easy city to navigate, being built across the looping confluence of the Saône and Rhône rivers, with hills on either side and a peninsula in the middle. A street map is essential (available at the tourist office on **place Bellecour**, in the middle of the Presqu'île, the peninsula between the two rivers).

Cross over the Pont Bonaparte to view the **Cathédrale St-Jean** and its astronomical clock, then stroll around the fine Renaissance houses of Lyon's **old town** between the Saône river and Fourvière hill. Some of the best examples are found along rues St-Georges, St-Jean, du Bœuf and Juiverie. In the handsome **Hôtel de Gadagne** (rue du Boeuf) there are two museums (www.gadagne-lyon.fr; both Wed–Sun 11am–6pm)**, Musée d'Histoire de Lyon,** recounting the history of Lyon (from the Middle Ages to the 19th century) and **Musée des Marionnettes du Monde**, which displays over 2,000 puppets from the town's celebrated *Théâtre Guignol* and beyond.

Further west, off rue de l'Antiquaille, are two important Roman **amphitheatres**, still used today, and the attractive **Musée de la Civilisation Gallo-Romaine** (corner of rue Cléberg; lugdunum.grand-lyon.com; Tue–Fri 11am–6pm, Sat–Sun opens at 10am), which houses a collection of statues, mosaics, coins and tools.

Rising over the old city is the elaborate late-19th-century **Basilique Notre-Dame-de-Fourvière**, which has four towers and various adorn-ments. Take the funicular railway from place St-Jean up to the top of the hill and walk down the **chemin du Rosaire**, with spectacular views of the town.

All of this will work up an appetite, easily satisfied in the restaurants and cafés of the old town or the Presqu'île, or perhaps the daily market on quais des Célestins and St-Antoine. Shoppers may want to visit the lively rue de la République and the streets around place des Jacobins.

Lyon has a wealth of museums, among which the following are worth a visit. The **Musée des Beaux-Arts** (20 place des Terreaux; www.

mba-lyon.fr; Wed–Mon 10am–6pm, Fri 10.30am–6pm), housed in a fine 17th-century Benedictine abbey, has a rich collection of European paintings and sculpture. Among the most notable are three Rodin bronzes in its cloister and works by Perugino, Veronese, Rubens, Monet, Degas, Gaugin and Picasso. The **Musée des Arts Décoratifs** (30 rue de la Charité; closed for renovation), in the 18th-century **Hôtel Lacroix-Laval**, displays tapestries, furniture and porcelain. Next door, in the **Hôtel Villeroy**, is the **Musée Historique des Tissus** (closed for renovation), showcasing tapestries, silks and other fabrics.

AUVERGNE

To the west of Lyon you will find one of the most naturally beautiful regions of France – and one of the quietest too. As well as providing a plethora of outdoor activities, the **Auvergne** offers historic castles, Romanesque churches, picture-postcard villages and its own unique cuisine. But it is for its spectacular volcanic landscape, in the heart of the Massif Central, that it is most famed. The **Chaine des Puys** stretches over 30km (19 miles) at the centre of the **Parc Naturel des Volcans d'Auvergne**. With some 80 domes and craters it is an open book for those interested in volcanoes and a magnificent environment for hiking.

The region is awash with natural lakes, rivers, ponds and waterfalls. The opportunities for water sports are incredible. The Auvergne boasts ten spa towns each renowned for its pure therapeutic waters and built around natural thermal springs. At the heart of the Massif Central is the historic town of **Le Puy-en-Velay** ㊷, famous as a starting point for pilgrims en route for Santiago de Compostela in Spain, and a lovely place to wander. You can't miss the Chapel Saint-Michel D'Aiguilhe, perched high on a rocky pinnacle.

PROVENCE

Most people approach Provence from the north; the warmth of the sun, the red-tiled roofs, the cypress trees, the *garrigue* (scrubland) and the fragrance of lavender alert you to the fact that you have arrived. Apart from the flat, well-populated coastal area, much of Provence is hilly, with small towns and villages that seem unchanged by the passage of time. Women dressed in black chat outside their houses; the men gather in shady squares to discuss the day's news and play *pétanque,* or *boules* (see page 207).

Provence has a history as rich as its soil; the monuments of the Roman Empire still stand proudly in Orange, Arles and Nîmes, as do the medieval strongholds in Les Baux and Avignon. But the most important pleasure of Provence is not the sightseeing but the leisurely pace of life, the sun-soaked landscape and the wonderful cuisine.

Provence bristles with cultural activity in the summer months, each town using its ancient amphitheatre *(arènes),* cathedral or palace as a magnificent setting for festivals of music, theatre and other performing arts (see page 217).

The itinerary we propose deals in turn with the various layers of Provençal life: the Roman towns of Orange, Vaison-la-Romaine, Nîmes

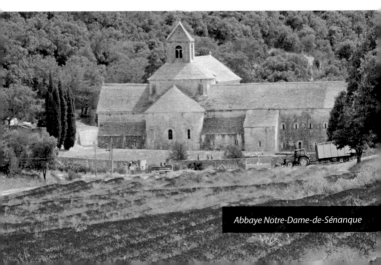

Abbaye Notre-Dame-de-Sénanque

Pont du Gard, one of the finest remaining Roman aqueducts in the world

and Arles; the medieval bastions of Les Baux and Avignon; the ancient villages of the Lubéron mountains; and, finally, the vibrant streets of Aix-en-Provence.

Orange

If your mind is leaping to images of orange groves in rocky valleys, think again. The name actually comes from the Royal Dutch House of Orange, who inherited the city in 1559 from the Chalon family. Since **Orange** 🅺 is the gateway to Provence, make an appropriate entrance into town from the north, at the imposing triumphal arch. Erected in AD 21, it stands on a traffic island across the old N7 (now the D907), which here traces the route of the ancient Via Agrippa. The friezes on the northern side, depicting battle scenes, weaponry and naval equipment, celebrate Julius Caesar's victories over the Gallic tribes of the region and the merchant fleet of the Greek colony in Marseilles.

The town's other great Roman monument, the **théâtre antique**, is on the south side of town. Historians regard this as the finest and best preserved of all the surviving theatres in the Roman Empire, unique for its towering scenic wall, with a statue of Emperor Augustus to greet you. In Roman times, some 10,000 spectators would gather here to watch a circus, Greek tragedy, Latin comedy or lottery draw. Today, the theatre still provides a wonderful setting for the July festival's opera and symphony concerts, although locals bring cushions to protect their *derrières* from the hard seats. From the top of the Colline St-Eutrope, you get a bird's-eye view of the theatre in relation to the triumphal arch and the Rhône Valley beyond.

After imagining yourself at a Roman circus, head for the **Musée d'Art et d'Histoire** (theatre-antique.com; daily June–Aug 9.15am–7pm, Apr–May and Sept 9.15am–6pm, Mar and Oct 9.45am–5.30pm, Nov–Feb 9.45am–noon 1pm–4.30pm), to see more Roman artefacts as well as the sections on the later history of Orange.

Vaison-la-Romaine

A pleasant drive 30km (19 miles) northeast of Orange along the D976 takes you to the site of one of the most important towns of Roman Provence, **Vaison-la-Romaine**. The Ouvèze river, spanned by a Roman bridge, separates the beautiful medieval *haute ville* (upper town) from the modern town and Roman ruins.

LOOKING FOR THE GHOST OF VAN GOGH

Van Gogh wrote in a letter from Arles: 'Oh, the beautiful sun of midsummer! It beats upon my head, and I do not doubt that it makes one a little queer.' It inspired his most fertile period, but also triggered the frenzy in which he cut off an ear and had himself committed to the asylum in nearby St-Rémy. A year later, he died after shooting himself.

Today, the tourist office in boulevard des Lices provides a map tracing 30 of the sites he painted while in Arles. His house and favourite café no longer exist, having been bombed in 1944. However, the sun is just as strong as ever, and amid the fields filled with sunflowers and olive trees you can still imagine the painter tramping the road to Tarascon.

Arles

The tourist magnets in this town are the archaeological digs in quartiers de Puymin and de la Villasse (www.vaison-la-romaine.com; daily, variable hours, tel: 04 90 36 02 11). On offer are excellent audio-guided tours of the ancient city, which sprawls over the surrounding hills. The on-site museum explains the layout of the ancient town, its streets, houses, shops, fountains and theatre, and displays some superb marble sculptures of the 2nd century AD, most notably of Venus, the Emperor Hadrian and his wife Sabina.

Pont du Gard

Take the A9 *autoroute* southwest from Orange to the Fournès-Remoulins exit, then follow the D981 to this gigantic 2,000-year-old **aqueduct**, without doubt the most impressive of all the Roman monuments preserved from ancient Gaul. It carried spring water from near Uzès to the town of Nîmes, a distance of 35km (22 miles).

Built of enormous granite blocks joined without mortar in three tiers of arches, six at the base, 11 at the middle level, and 35 at the top, this highly functional construction is also remarkably beautiful, in total harmony with its landscape. The best view is from the riverbank near the Château St-Privat, beyond the aqueduct.

Arles

For many connoisseurs, **Arles** *is* Provence. No other city is so aware of its heritage, locals here refer to themselves as *vrai* ('true') Provençals, and the so-called 'Queen of Arles' is selected on her understanding of Provençal customs and ability to speak the dialect rather than her beauty – or so the residents proudly assert. An important town in Roman Gaul, receiving the blessing of Caesar over Marseille as a port and replacing Lyon as capital towards the end of the Empire, Arles has a very well-preserved **amphitheatre**, which seated more than 20,000 spectators in the days of the gladiators. Today it is the site of bullfights and gladiator re-enactments. For the most magnificent view, climb up to the broad path that runs along the roof of the arches on its perimeter.

Less fortunate than the example at Orange, the Roman **théâtre antique** here has been reduced to ruins over the centuries, as builders carted away stone for their houses, churches and town walls – but the remains, in a pleasant park, recall its noble past, and its stage still hosts events today.

In the **Eglise St-Trophime** (place de la République), you can see the Roman influence recurring in the triumphal-arch design of its splendid porch. This masterpiece of Provençal Romanesque sculpture depicts the Last Judgment in the tympanum above the doors, surrounded by statues of the saints. Nearby, the church cloister, **Cloître St-Trophime**, with its beautiful sculpted capitals on the pillars, is a haven of peace.

To the southeast of the town, cut off by a railway track, you'll find the melancholy remains of the **Alyscamps**, the famous Roman and medieval burial grounds that were a favourite subject of Van Gogh when he came to live in Arles in 1888.

In the dramatic **Musée de l'Arles Antique** (avenue de la Première Division France Libre; Wed Mon 10am–6pm), lively exhibitions of Roman statues and early Christian sarcophagi with impressive architectural models bring the ancient city back to life.

The Camargue

At the delta of the Rhône, where its two arms spill into the Mediterranean, the **Parc de Camargue** ❹ has been reclaimed from the sea to form a nature reserve. The region is famous for its white horses, its bullfighting and for the wild ducks, herons and pink flamingos that gather here. There are relatively few roads through the Camargue, and those that do exist are not always very attractive. So, many people choose – despite the heat – to follow the many hiking and riding trails through the area.

The **Musée Camarguais** at **Albaron** gives a glimpse of the traditional lifestyle of the area, and sets you off on a 3.5-km (2-mile) guided walk through the marshland. The **Parc Ornithologique** at Pont de Gau allows you to watch a number of bird species without long hikes into the interior.

But the Camargue isn't just a remote haven for wildlife; despite the dearth of villages inland there are modern resorts along the coast, including the bustling **Stes-Maries-de-la-Mer** with its long, sandy beaches. The local tourist office will help you find organised tours into the interior on horseback, by boat or by jeep.

Les Baux-de-Provence

The astounding sight of the medieval citadel, clinging to a massive outcrop of rock cut adrift from the Alpilles mountains at **Les**

POPES AND ANTI-POPES

In 1309 Pope Clement V moved his Holy See to Avignon, in part to escape the turmoil of Rome and in part to pander to France's Philippe IV. Seven popes, all French, made their home beside the Rhône.

Like Rome, Avignon became a city of pomp and intrigue. It attracted great Italian artists, such as the poet Petrarch and Sienese painter Simone Martini, but was soon decried as 'an unholy Babylon' of gaudy luxury and vicious riff-raff. This was not at all to the liking of the pious mystic Catherine of Siena, who brought Pope Gregory XI back to Rome in 1377.

A year later, however, more power struggles resulted in Clement VII leaving Italy for Avignon and reigning as the first of a series of three rival 'anti-popes'. Forty years later the infighting ended and the papal court was reunited in Rome. Avignon itself remained part of the papal lands until the French Revolution.

Baux-de-Provence 45 takes your breath away. Officially acknowledged as one of the most beautiful villages in France, it is also one of the area's major tourist attractions and can be unpleasantly crowded in midsummer.

The feudal barons of Les Baux put the star of the Nativity on their coat of arms, claiming to be descendants of Balthazar, one of the Three Wise Men. They ruled medieval Provence, and their impregnable fortress

Avignon's Palais des Papes

became a centre of courtly love prized by travelling troubadours.

For centuries the barons defied the papal authority in Avignon and the kings of France, offering refuge to Protestants during the Wars of Religion until, in 1632, Louis XIII ordered the destruction of Les Baux. The demolition of the citadel was a half-hearted job, however, and there's plenty left to see today, from ramparts and castle walls to ruined chapels, stone stairways and quaint cobbled streets. Museums, art galleries and boutiques all add to the charm. Visit at sundown or out of season to get the full flavour of the setting. The nearby Carrières de Lumières uses a former limestone quarry as the backdrop for a stunning show of giant images, which film buffs will recognise as the site of Jean Cocteau's *Orpheus* and *Antigone*. The theme here changes each year.

Avignon

Erstwhile 'City of the Popes', **Avignon** 46 is today a proud cultural centre, home of one of Europe's greatest arts festivals, and a lively and cheerful town of good cafés, art galleries and fashionable shops. Seven popes reigned in Avignon from 1309 until 1377, followed by three renegade

Festival d'Avignon

Avignon's summer festival was established in 1947 by actor Jean Vilar and his Théâtre National Populaire to make the performing arts accessible to all. Productions include theatre from Racine to Ionesco and 'fringe' shows. There is also puppetry, dance, mime, orchestral concerts and café cabarets. For more details, visit www.festival-avignon.com.

popes. The **Palais des Papes** (www.palais-des-papes.com; daily 10am–7pm, book ahead) is the resulting combination of feudal fortress and opulent palace. During the Revolution, all evidence of luxury was stripped from the palace interior, but the structure itself proved stronger than its assailants and today it hosts major productions during the annual festival.

The enormous building is actually a series of connected palaces. The forbidding design of the Palais Vieux, reflecting the pious austerity of Benedict XII, contrasts with successor Clement VI's more decorative Palais Nouveau. Frescoes adorn many palace chambers, among them works by Simone Martini, brought from the porch of Notre-Dame des Doms cathedral. The Petit Palais, at the northern end of place du Palais, displays a fine collection of Italian painting from the 13th to 16th centuries, including major works by Taddeo Gaddi, Veneziano, Botticelli and Carpaccio's *Holy Conversation*.

North of the palace, beyond the much-remodelled cathedral, is the pleasant garden of the **Rocher des Doms**, which extends to the outer ramparts. From here you will get your best view of the **Pont d'Avignon** – more correctly called the Pont St-Bénézet – broken off halfway across the Rhône river. Despite the words of the song *Sur le Pont d'Avignon* (On Avignon Bridge), the dancers actually used to perform *under* the bridge, on a little island.

There are several museums in Avignon, the most enchanting of which is the Musée Angladon (5 rue Laboureur; www.angladon.com; Tue–Sat 1–6pm, also Sun Apr–Sept) presents an exceptional private art collection including many 19th- and 20th-century masterpieces by artists including Picasso, Cézanne, Van Gogh, Modigliani, Manet and Degas. In the centre of town the airy **place de l'Horloge**, is surrounded by cafés and a pedestrian shopping zone along rue des Marchands. At the far end are place Jérusalem and a 19th-century synagogue built on the site of one dating from the Middle Ages and destroyed by fire.

For an interesting walk through the **old town**, start at the 14th-century **Eglise St-Didier**, with its altar sculpture of *Jesus Carrying the Cross* by the Dalmatian artist Francesco Laurana. Rue du Roi-René will take you past some handsome 17th- and 18th-century houses and on to the pretty, cobblestoned rue des Teinturiers; here you can see where the dyers used to work the paddlewheels for their Indian-style cloth in the little Sorgue river, emerging here from its underground course.

The Lubéron and Vaucluse

Starting out from **Cavaillon** 47, home of famously succulent cantaloupe melons, head east to the Lubéron mountains, the heart of the Provençal

Village on the outskirts of Avignon

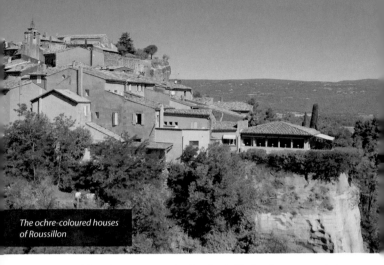

The ochre-coloured houses of Roussillon

countryside and now a protected regional park. Whole valleys are carpeted with lavender, and the *garrigue* scrubland shimmers with every colour and fragrance of the sunny Mediterranean. Many villages here, which are known as *villages perchés*, or hilltop villages, have been lovingly restored.

Perched on a spur of rock, the village of **Oppède-le-Vieux** has been rescued from its ruins by writers and artists seeking a residence off the beaten track. **Ménerbes** is also perched on a hill, with a medieval citadel that served as the Protestants' last redoubt in the 16th-century Wars of Religion. Behind the church on the outskirts of town there is a magnificent view over the mountains to the Vaucluse plateau and the distant peak of Mont Ventoux, a popular subject of the painter Cézanne.

Bonnieux juts out over the Coulon Valley. From the hillside terrace behind the town hall, look northwest to the rust-coloured ravines surrounding **Roussillon**. In order to set off that startling red, the villagers of Roussillon paint their houses with every imaginable variation of ochre from the neighbouring quarries.

A dramatic location, looking across to the Lubéron from the southern edge of the Vaucluse plateau, has made **Gordes** one of the region's most prosperous villages, popular for its boutiques and little galleries. Its houses hug the hillside, on steep, winding streets, leading to a 16th-century castle at the top. Approximately 2km (1 mile) southwest of Gordes is the strange little **Village des Bories.** The *bories* are old dry-stone cabins that are grouped around a baker's oven and serving as a museum of rural life in Provence.

Aix-en-Provence

The first Roman town in Gaul (a citadel and spa founded in 125BC as Aquae Sextiae), contemporary **Aix-en-Provence ⑱** is elegant, cultured and attractive. The town's great treasure is its main thoroughfare, cours Mirabeau, lined with plane trees and dotted with fountains. When in Aix, look out for *calissons,* the local delicacy made from ground almonds, candied melon and oranges.

People still come to Aix to take the waters – the moss-covered fountain in the middle of cours Mirabeau spurts water with a natural temperature of 34°C (93.2°F). But the town's renowned university keeps the spirit of the town young and cosmopolitan. You'll find fountains and squares scattered over the old town north of cours Mirabeau, one of the most attractive being the tranquil **place d'Albertas**.

The cathedral, on place d'Albertas, is less worthy of your attention than its exquisite little Romanesque **Cloître St-Sauveur**. Chamber music and choral recitals are held there during Aix's summer music festival; operas are performed behind the cloister, in the Palais de l'Ancien Archevêché.

Paul Cézanne spent most of his life in Aix, and his studio (9 avenue Paul-Cézanne) has been preserved as a **museum** (www.atelier-cezanne. com; daily Jun–Sep 9.30am–6pm, Apr–May 9.30am–12.30pm 2–6pm, Oct–Mar 9.30am–12.30pm, 2–5pm, closed Sun and Mon Oct–Mar), which includes his palette and other belongings. But the best way to evoke his memory is to drive out to the subject of his most famous landscapes, **Montagne Ste-Victoire**, just 14 km (9 miles) east of Aix on the D10.

Filleting fish in Marseille

MA 308327

THE CÔTE D'AZUR

When the British discovered this playground in the 19th century, they called it the French Riviera, distinguishing it from the Italian one that starts round the corner at Ventimiglia. Nowadays, it's considered more chic to use its French name, the Côte d'Azur.

In summer the area tends to be somewhat overcrowded, but that's part of the fun. You can always head away from the coast and into the hills of Provence for some peace. Most of the beaches are fabulous; the young people are beautiful, and even the older crowd makes for entertaining people-watching. And over the years a string of A-listers have owned houses here, from icons such as Matisse and Picasso to Wallis Simpson and Brigitte Bardot. Fine weather, with hot days and balmy nights, is almost guaranteed, and apart from the occasional unsightly apartment block, the coastline outside the resorts has considerable charm. The native umbrella pines share the landscape with acacia, eucalyptus and palm trees imported by British gardeners.

Purists say that the Côte d'Azur reaches from Cannes to Menton, including only the original, more exclusive resort towns of Juan-les-Pins,

Antibes, Nice and Monte-Carlo. However, in recent years the tourist industry has extended the 'Côte' westward to include popular family-style resorts such as St-Raphaël and Ste-Maxime and the ultra-glamorous St-Tropez. Marseille may not strictly qualify for inclusion, but this tough and gritty metropolis is hard to overlook – particularly if you like *bouillabaisse*, a delicious seafood stew and local speciality.

Marseille

A noisy, boisterous, multicultural port, **Marseille** 49 is not a typical French tourist destination. But France's oldest city, founded by Greek colonists over 2,500 years ago, should not be ignored. It has worked hard to rid Itself of its seedy image as a centre of corruption and drug trafficking, and vast renovations in both the city and the port have resulted in a surge in the number of cruise visitors. Cultural newcomers are the Musée des Civilisations de l'Europe et de la Méditerranée (www.mucem.org), a vast museum and exhibition space, plus theatre, cinema and concert space. The Cosquer Méditerrannée opened in 2022 alongside the MuCem, and is an ambitious replica of the Grotte Cosquer in the Morgiou calanque just south of the city. The cave and the 500 prehistoric drawings it houses were discovered in 1985 by diver Henri Cosquer.

The main thoroughfare, **La Canebière**, will give you a taste of the city's heady atmosphere. Explore further and you will find a wide variety of urban landscapes, from peaceful squares and parks to the narrow streets and steep stairs of the medieval **Panier** district, which make you feel as if you have left France altogether. The Tourist Bureau (11 La Canebière; www.marseille-tourisme.com)

Daughter of the sea

'What an enchanting and simple daughter of the sea! You can smell the fish, the burning tar, the brine. The scales of sardines glitter on the cobblestones like pearls.' Guy de Maupassant might weary of the traffic in modern St-Tropez, but he would still appreciate the resort's beauty.

supplies maps with routes to explore the old city on foot; there is also an innovative tour conducted in air-conditioned taxis equipped with recorded cassettes (known as *Taxi-Tourisme*).

The **Vieux Port** (old port) marks the spot where Phocaean-Greek merchants from Asia Minor docked to create their Western Mediterranean trading post. Today, it's a colourful harbour for yachts and motorboats and the site of a lively daily fish market. From quai des Belges, you can take a cruise out to the **Château d'If**, the island prison that was the scene of Alexandre Dumas's *Count of Monte Cristo*.

To the south of the old port, the 19th-century basilica of **Notre-Dame-de-la-Garde** offers an amazing view over the city, the Mediterranean and the mountains inland. East of Marseille are several rugged, narrow inlets called *calanques* – favourites of hikers, mountain climbers, scuba divers, cliff divers, yachters, swimmers and birdwatchers. It is possible to take local buses from Marseille or you can take one of the frequent boat tours from the alluring town of **Cassis**, about 20km (12 miles) away, but new regulations concerning numbers of visitors to the most accessible calanques are now in effect as the region looks to preserve this incredible environment.

St-Tropez

The lovely town of **St-Tropez** ⑤⓪ is alone on the Riviera in facing north-wards, which gives a special quality to the evening sunlight as it reflects off the dull-pink and ochre walls of many of the buildings. Made fashionable by the film stars in the 1950s, St-Tropez has retained its popularity with fashion photographers, models and groupies of the good life. The essence of St-Tropez has always been the parade of people along the **Vieux Port** (old port) in fashionable boutiques, on chic yachts and at hip cafés.

You won't find many masterpieces among the offerings of the harbourside artists, but the **Musée de l'Annonciade** (place Charles-Grammont; Apr–Oct daily 10am–6pm, July–Sept until 7pm, Nov–Mar Tue–Sun 10am–5pm) has an outstanding collection of paintings from 1890 to 1940 – many of them studies of St-Tropez itself. Housed in a renovated 16th-century chapel with natural Mediterranean light, they include important works by Bonnard, Derain, Van Dongen, Matisse, Signac and Braque.

Away from the harbourside, the town keeps its Provençal character intact on **place des Lices**, nicely shaded by plane trees for the Tuesday and Saturday morning markets, a late-afternoon game of *boules* or a sunset apéritif. For a view over the port, climb up to the 16th-century **citadel**, built to defend the town on a coast under constant attack from pirates. Drive out of town south along the D93, signposted

The St-Tropez quayside

Cannes seafront

Route des Plages, to Tahiti or Pampelonne for the best **beaches**, which have fine sand shaded by umbrella pines.

Cannes to Biot

'Princes, princes, nothing but princes', groaned Guy de Maupassant, who frequently sailed in the bay around **Cannes ⑤**. 'If you like them, you're in the right place.' This luxury resort gave the nobility of Europe, headed by the ex-Chancellor of the Bank of England Lord Brougham in 1834, the opportunity to realise their wildest dreams. Cannes still offers a magnificent beachfront, the most elegant of boutiques and jewellery shops and the grandest hotels.

Overlooking fine white-sand beaches, **La Croisette** is Cannes's grand palm tree-lined promenade, which runs past the great hotels to the old port and the gigantic **Palais des Festivals**. This last is the venue of the international film festival in May and the recorded music festival (MIDEM) in January. If you don't mind crowds, both these festivals offer plenty of opportunities to stare at the stars.

Up on the hill, overlooking the port, **Le Suquet** preserves something of the old fishing village and gives you a fine view of the coast. This may whet your appetite for a boat cruise (from the port's Gare Maritime) to the **Iles des Lérins**, where you can stroll through eucalyptus groves and beautiful flower gardens.

Just east of Cannes are two towns renowned for their craftwork. At **Vallauris** the ceramics and pottery industry was revived almost single-handedly by Picasso, who worked in the town after World War II. He also decorated its Romanesque chapel with murals entitled _La Guerre et la Paix_

(War and Peace) and left a bronze sculpture on the place Paul-Isnard. **Biot** – certainly worth visiting for its well-preserved 16th-century centre – is widely reputed for its tinted glassware characterised by delicate bubbles.

St-Paul-de-Vence

The feudal fortified village of **St-Paul-de-Vence,** up behind Cagnes-sur-Mer, is situated amid colourful terraces of vines, bougainvillea and mimosa, guarded by tall cypresses. It was discovered in the 1920s by painters such as Signac, Bonnard and Modigliani, who lived in the *auberge* (hostel) at the entrance to the village and paid with their paint-ings. They were joined by artists such as Matisse, Camus and Kipling to create a sort of Saint-Germain-des-Prés-de-la-Mer. The curse of beauty the world over brought first the movie crowd in the 1940s and then the tourists to this 'refuge'.

It's still unmissable though, even in crowded mid-summer, for its stone houses, little squares and the sense of artistic history. To enjoy the view over the valley, have a drink on the terrace of the renowned **Colombe d'Or** restaurant. If you stay for dinner, you'll be able to inspect the restaurant's famous collection of paintings by Matisse, Derain and Utrillo.

An even more impres-sive collection of modern art awaits you at the splendid **Fondation Maeght** (Montée des Trious; www.fondation-maeght.com; closed for exten-sion works, reopening July 2023), located on a grassy hill just outside the town. Here you'll find an imposing black

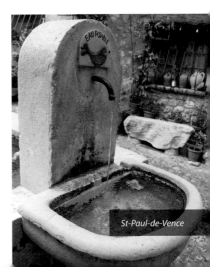

St-Paul-de-Vence

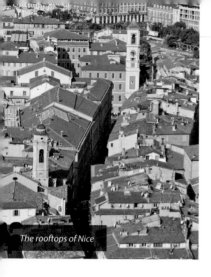
The rooftops of Nice

sculpture by Alexander Calder at the entrance, some monumental pieces by Miró in the gardens and a matchless array of Giacometti statues in the beautiful courtyard.

Nice

An ancient Greek trading post, **Nice** 52 manages to combine the atmosphere of a resort with a gutsy, bustling city life and was inscripted as a UNESCO World Heritage City in summer 2021. The tempting shops and first-class restaurants more than make up for the crowded pebble beach. Natives and visitors alike stroll on the grand **Promenade des Anglais**, financed by the town's English colony in 1822 to replace a little footpath. The most remarkable landmark on this waterfront is a masterpiece of Belle Epoque wedding-cake architecture, the pink-domed **Hôtel Negresco**. The promenade terminates with a spectacular display of flowers and fountains in the **Jardin Albert I**.

The **vieille ville** (old town), whose architecture shows the town's long relationship with Italy, is now the home of many art galleries and boutiques. The daily market in **cours Saleya** will whet your appetite for the fare at the surrounding cafés and restaurants.

On the northeastern edge of the old town is the **Musée d'Art Moderne et d'Art Contemporain** (MAMAC; www.mamac-nice.org; Tue–Sun 10am–6pm, Nov–Apr opens at 11am), the spacious home to an excellent collection of works by modern and contemporary artists including the 'Nice School' – Yves Klein, Martial Raysse, César and Ben. Just opposite the museum is the city's main theatre.

For a good view over the port, the Baie des Anges and the mountain backdrop, climb up to the little park on top of the hill still known as **Le Château**, even though its castle was destroyed centuries ago. The ruins you can see there now are the remains of the 11th-century cathedral.

The fashionable residential **Cimiez** district sits on the hills outside the centre and offers a quiet interlude from the busy streets. In addition to a large park you will find the Franciscan **Monastère Cimiez** (place du Monastère), where Matisse is buried, a museum of religious art, the **Musée Matisse** (164 avenue des Arènes de Cimiez; www.musee-matisse-nice.org; Wed–Mon 10am–6pm, Nov–Apr closes at 5pm) and the **Musée et Site Archéologique** (164 avenue des Arènes de Cimiez; www.musee-archeologie-nice.org; Wed–Mon 10am–6pm, Nov–Apr closes at 5pm), next to the remains of Roman baths and amphitheatre.

Les Corniches

The route from Nice to Monaco, along the precipices of the Maritime Alps' southern slopes, offers one of the most spectacular drives in the country. There are three winding roads, or *corniches*: the *Grande,* the high road, starting out from the Avenue des Diables-Bleus in Nice; the *Moyenne,* or middle road, beginning at Place Max-Barel and the most photogenic (as well as the most precipitous – Princess Grace of Monaco died in a car crash here in 1982) and the Basse, along the coast from Boulevard Carnot, but usually jammed with traffic. Above them all is the *autoroute.*

The **Grande Corniche** follows the route of the ancient Roman road, Via Aurelia. Stop off at **Belvédère d'Eze** and **La Turbie** for great views of the coast, especially the lights of Monaco at night. In La Turbie, climb up to the remains of a curious 2,000-year-old Roman monument – the towering **Trophée des Alpes**, erected by Emperor Augustus to commemorate victories over the Gallic tribes named in the inscription on the base.

The highlight of the **Moyenne Corniche** is the hilltop village of **Eze**. Hanging at a dizzying angle above the sea, it was once the fortress of Ligurian brigands. In summer it's a bit of a tourist trap, but worth a visit for the cacti and tropical flowers (plus ruins of a 14th-century castle) in the **Jardin Exotique**. Its terrace affords the best (although not free) view of the coast.

The pretty hillside town of **Villefranche-sur-Mer** is a good base for exploring the area, particularly for families with children. The deepwater port allows cruise ships to anchor, so the sandy beaches and colourful waterfront cafés and restaurants can become quite crowded. But if you climb the maze of steep narrow streets into the upper part, you'll find peaceful, shady squares. Jean Cocteau decorated the little **Chapelle St-Pierre** (quai Courbet) with modern frescoes in 1957. Rue Oscura is the most impressive of the ancient vaulted passages.

Within easy reach of Villefranche are the resorts of St-Jean Cap Ferrat, Beaulieu, **La Turbie** (named after the monument erected between 13 and 5BC to commemorate the conquest of the 45 Alpine tribes who had been attacking Romanised Gaul) and Roquebrune-Cap Martin. Also nearby is **Menton**, famed for its lemon festival and its link with Surrealist Jean Cocteau. The room used to conduct marriage ceremonies

Menton is famous for its lemon festival

in the Hôtel de Ville (Town Hall) was decorated with murals by Cocteau in the 1950s, and in a 17th-century fort on quai Monléon, by the harbour, is the Musée Jean Cocteau (www. museecocteaumenton.fr; daily 10am–12.30pm 2–6pm).

Monaco

Between the 1870s and 1930s, changing laws and fashions made **Monte-Carlo** the roulette capital of Europe, and the wintering place of the very rich and of mothers with eligible daughters. More recently, the late Prince Rainier III diversified his economic base by turning the tiny country of **Monaco** ⑤ into the Miami of the Mediterranean. Sea, skyscrapers and mountains form concentric circles around the tiny headland that is Monaco. Like many Americans in 1956, Mrs Kelly is said to have believed her daughter was engaged to the Prince of Morocco. Tourism in Monaco doubled within a few years of film star Grace Kelly's televised wedding in the Cathédrale St Nicholas on Le Rocher.

Sights include the **Musée Océanographique** (musee.oceano.org; daily July–Aug 9.30am–8pm Apr–June, Sept 10am–7pm, Oct Mar 10am–6pm) and the **Palais des Princes**, the royal family's official residence. The museum celebrated its 100th anniversary in 2010 having completed extensive renovations. From the Palace, where a daily changing of the guard is still performed at 11.55am, a stroll through the old quarter leads to the cathedral and Jardin Exotique (daily).

A desolate town

In the 1920s Sir Frederick Treves, in the *Riviera of the Corniche Road*, described Eze: 'It is a silent town and desolate. On the occasion of a certain visit the only occupant I came upon was a half-demented beggar who gibbered in an unknown tongue.' Nowadays, the village is considerably more popular.

CORSICA

The rugged, unspoiled island of **Corsica** offers dramatic coastlines and a wild interior of densely forested hills. The population of under a quarter

Calvi, one of Corsica's most
popular seaside resorts

of a million is concentrated mainly in the two major towns of Bastia
(industrial and noisy, but with a colourful old town) and the more attractive Ajaccio. You can alternate lazy days on the beach with some of the
Mediterranean's best deep-sea diving, boat excursions around pirate
coves, canoeing and fishing on inland rivers, or hikes and picnics in the
mountains. For the sun-seeker, the best seaside resorts are along the
indented shorelines of the west and south coasts, for which Ajaccio's
airport and harbour (for the car ferry from Nice, Toulon or Marseille) provide a convenient gateway. Give yourself plenty of driving time, as the
roads are narrow and tortuous.

Ajaccio

At the head of the Gulf of **Ajaccio** ⑤④, Napoleon's birthplace is the liveliest of Corsican towns, but tourists impatient to get out to the seaside
resorts are usually content with a stroll around the port and a pilgrimage
to the **Maison Bonaparte** (rue St-Charles; Tue–Sun Apr–Sept 10.30am–
12.30pm, 1.15–5.30pm, Oct–Mar 10.30am–12.30pm, 1.15–4.30pm).
An audio tour of the house will tell you how, on Assumption Day (15

August) of 1769, Napoleon's mother Letizia was rushed out of church with her first birth pains. She made it no further than a first-floor sofa to bring little Nabulio kicking and screaming into the world he was to conquer. The sofa you see there now is a replica, the original having been stolen during the Revolution. South of Ajaccio, the major seaside resorts are **Porticcio** and **Propriano**, both with sandy beaches and good opportunities for sailing and deep-sea diving.

Bonifacio

The best way to approach the proud old town of **Bonifacio** ⑮ perched high on the cliffs is by boat, past the limpid blue waters of the **Sdragonato cave** and the **Escalier du Roi d'Aragon**, a staircase cut diagonally into the cliff face, used by the soldiers of the Spanish king in an abortive siege of the town in the 15th century. When you are visiting the old town, enjoy the exhilarating walk down the staircase to the base of the cliffs and along the water's edge.

Porto-Vecchio

Surrounded by a pretty forest of cork oaks and sweet-smelling eucalyptus, the gulf surrounding **Porto-Vecchio** ⑯ has an ever-expanding series of luxury resorts, the best being out on the fine sandy beaches of **Cala Rossa**. Inland, there are some particularly beautiful excursions to be made into the forests of **l'Ospedale** and **Zonza**. The cork oaks are stripped of their valuable bark every ten years, baring a russet-brown trunk until the cork grows back again.

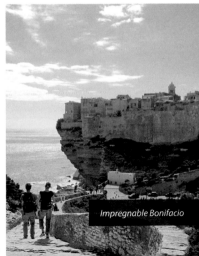

Impregnable Bonifacio

For a memorable picnic up on the lovely wild mountain pass of **Bavella**, take some of the delicious Corsican tomatoes, smoked liver sausage *(figatelli)* and ewe's or goat's milk cheese *(broccio)*. Be careful with the heady Corsican wine, as it's stronger than you might expect.

Golfe de Porto

Some of France's most grandiose panoramas of sea and landscape are clustered around the **Golfe de Porto**, 70km (43 miles) north of Ajaccio. **Piana 57** is the most delightful of the gulf's sleepy village resorts, a place unspoiled by commercialisation and blessed with the nearby natural wonders of **Capo Rosso** and the **Calanche**. These rugged red-granite cliffs and boulders have been hurled down to the sea by volcanic eruptions and eroded there by wind and water, forming the most bizarre and fantastic shapes. Take the walk on **chemin du Château-Fort** to admire them.

Don't miss taking a **boat cruise** from the little resort town of Porto. The best one goes out to the cliff caves on the northern edge of the gulf, to the isolated fishing village of **Girolata** and the nature reserve of **Scandola** – a marvellous coastal haven for eagles, bald buzzards and other rare species nesting on the peaks of the volcanic rocks.

In the interior, drive along the winding mountain road to Evisa and the cool, quiet **Fôret d'Aïtone**. Off the D84 road, just 3km (2 miles) northeast of Evisa, is a sign reading *Piscine* (swimming pool). This is not a municipal chlorine-saturated pool, but a series of clear, natural ones formed in smooth slabs of rock by the waterfalls known as the **Cascades d'Aïtone** – and a sheer delight.

THE SOUTHWEST

The area extending from the southern edge of the Loire Valley to the Pyrenees and the Atlantic coast into the Massif Central and southern Mediterranean coast encompasses a variety of terrains. In and around the Dordogne valley is Périgord, with its rich cuisine, fortified towns and fascinating cave paintings. Below the Loire estuary, the Atlantic coast is the preserve of the country's most independent-minded ports, the Protestant stronghold of La Rochelle and the prosperous city of Bordeaux. From the Basque country to the Mediterranean, you can explore the Pyrenees. And in between are the historic towns of Toulouse, Albi and Montpellier.

BERRY-LIMOUSIN

Many visitors driving from Paris to the Dordogne and Toulouse speed through this area on the *autoroute,* missing some pleasant countryside and towns. Among the stops to consider are Bourges, Limoges and Uzerche.

Bourges

Ancient capital of the flat region of Berry on the northern edge of Périgord close to the Loire, **Bourges** 58 is on the road south to

Pyrénées horses waiting for a 'promenade' in the cirque de Gavarnie

Clermont-Ferrand and Montpellier but is worth a brief detour for those using the A20.

The intricate harmony of the five portals of its facade and the peculiar grace of its silhouette make Bourges's Unesco-protected **Cathédrale de St-Etienne** (www.bourges-cathedrale.fr; daily May–Aug 9.30–11.30am, 2–5.45pm Sun 2–5.45pm, rest of year slightly shorter hours) a Gothic masterpiece. The church is dominated by the massive nave and flying buttresses linking the five chapels to the chancel. The best view is from the archbishop's gardens behind the cathedral. The Last Judgment portrayed on the central portal shows 13th-century sculpture at its best.

The **Palais Jacques-Cœur** (www.palais-jacques-coeur.fr; daily variable hours, check website), a rare example of Gothic secular architecture, was the residence of the treasurer to Charles VII. The elegance of the palace becomes apparent only in the inner courtyard, with its seven turreted staircases and handsome balconies. The mottos engraved around the windows proclaim the self-made man: *A vaillans (cœurs) riens impossible* (To valiant hearts, nothing is impossible) and *Dire, faire, taire* (Say, do, and be silent). Note the pigeon loft from which, 400 years before Reuters, Jacques Cœur organised a private news service using carrier pigeons.

During the tourist season splendid illuminations make exploring Bourges in the evenings a pleasure. The cathedral in particular is impressive after dark.

Limoges

The city of **Limoges** ⑩ is known for its porcelain and enamel, and still produces a major portion of France's tableware. The 18th-century **Musée Municipal de l'Evêché** (place de la Cathédrale; http://www.museebal.fr; Wed–Mon 9.30am–noon 2–5pm, closed Sun morning) has an enamel museum as well as a lapidary collection and a handful of paintings by Renoir, who was born in Limoges. The **Musée National de la Porcelaine Adrien Dubouché** (place Winston Churchill; www.musee-adriendubouche.fr; Wed–Mon 10am–12.30pm, 2–5.45pm) traces

The picture-postcard town of Uzerche

the history of pottery, china, stoneware and porcelain, with as many as 12,000 items on display.

Other sights in Limoges include its **Cathédrale St-Etienne**, a Gothic masterpiece that took 600 years to complete, and the part of the upper town, or *haute ville* (also called the Château), that contains the ancient **rue de la Boucherie** and pretty **cour du Temple**. There are pleasant walks along the banks of the river Vienne.

Uzerche

The 'Pearl of Limousin' **Uzerche** consists of an impressive collection of slate-roofed turrets and towers rising high above the Vézère river. A fortified town that withstood many sieges in the Middle Ages, Uzerche later became a favourite of prosperous families who built manor houses on the steep slopes. Among the structures of note are the ancient **Porte Bécharie** and **Tour du Prince**, the Romanesque **Eglise St-Pierre** with its 11th-century crypt and the Renaissance **Hôtel d'Eyssartier** (place de la Libération). Lorries on the *route nationale* used to roar through the narrow main street, but since construction of the *autoroute* Uzerche has again become a peaceful place in which to stroll. **L'Esplanade de la Lunade** provides a great view down to the river below.

PÉRIGORD

This rich and fertile country is densely forested and crisscrossed by rivers flowing from the plateau of the Massif Central out to the Atlantic Ocean. Of these, the Dordogne has carved a particularly beautiful winding valley of gentle greenery.

The village markets groan with fruits and vegetables, mushrooms and nuts of every description. Truffles, pâté de foie gras and slowly roasted *confit* of goose and duck are specialities, as are wild mushrooms, dried and smoked pork and walnut oil.

Stone-Age people found abundant fish in the rivers and dwellings safe from wild animals in the caves riddling the valley cliffs. With a similar concern for self-protection, the many fortresses throughout the Périgord region bear witness to the wars against the English, between Protestant and Catholic, and the resistance to the marauding bands of brigands.

Vallée de la Vézère

Exploring the valley that shelters the earliest signs of European civilisation is by no means a dry and dusty archaeological tour of fossils and bones. Children who are suffering from an overload of art and architecture will enjoy the caves with their stalactites and stalagmites, as well as the exhibits and zoo at Le Thot. Both adults and children alike will appreciate the hanging cliffs and attractive countryside of meadows, vineyards and orchards.

Montignac ❻ is the departure point for visits to the world-famous cave paintings of **Lascaux**. Concealed and protected against atmospheric changes for 17,000 years, these awe-inspiring frescoes and engravings of bulls, horses, ibex, bison and deer were discovered by four teenagers chasing a dog in 1940.

Within a few years, the carbon dioxide generated by the crowds of visitors caused a rapid deterioration in the cave walls, and the caves

had to be closed to the general public. Lascaux 4 was opened in 2016, a stunning full-scale replica of the world-famous cave housed in a low-lying super-modern building. Anthropologists and artists have reproduced the Painted Gallery and the Hall of Bulls *(Salle des Taureaux),* which contains 100 pictures of the animals. Complete your visit with a detour to **Le Thot** (www.parc-thot.fr; tel: 05 53 51 95 03; summer daily, winter Tue–Sun variable hours; call ahead), where the museum has excellent audiovisual exhibits and models of cave life; the nearby park has been turned into a zoo for descendants of the animals portrayed at Lascaux.

Returning to the river, you will pass the 16th-century **Château de Losse** (where visitors can admire Renaissance furniture and tapestries) on the way to **St-Léon-sur-Vézère**. Surrounded by poplars and willows, the town's buff-stoned 11th-century church is characteristic of Périgord Romanesque.

For a wonderful view of the valley, climb to the top of **La Roque St-Christophe**, a spectacular cliff 80m (262ft) high, honeycombed with caves with traces of troglodytic life.

Les Eyzies-de-Tayac is known as *capitale de la préhistoire.* Besides its **museum** (musee-prehistoire-eyzies.fr; July–Aug daily 9.30am–6.30pm, June and Sept Wed–Mon 9.30am–6pm, Oct–May Wed–Mon 9.30am–12.30pm, 2–5.30pm) in the remains of a medieval castle, the village is at the centre of dozens of major palaeolithic excavation sites. The Cro-Magnon shelter *(Abri de Cro-Magnon)* on the north side of town is the spot where, in 1868, railway workers uncovered three 30,000-year-old human skeletons beside their flint and bone tools.

The most attractive cave-painting site is the **Grotte de Font-de-Gaume** (www.sites-les-eyzies.fr; tel: 05 53 06 86 00; Mon–Fri and Sun; mid-May–mid-Sept 9.30am–5.30pm, mid-Sept–mid-May 9.30am–12.30pm, 2–5.30pm; online reservations required), reached by an easy walk up on a cliff above the eastern edge of town. The pictures of mammoths, bison, horses and reindeer are between 15,000 and 40,000 years old. The **Combarelles** cave (www.sites-les-eyzies.fr; same hours; online reservation required), to the east, is a winding gallery where the pictures are engraved rather than painted, and often superimposed.

The caverns of the **Grotte du Grand Roc**, to the northwest of Les Eyzies, are a natural rather than a historical phenomenon, but worth a

STONE-AGE ART

No household tools or weapons were found near the paintings, so scholars have deduced that most of the caves were not dwellings, but sanctuaries where Stone-Age man depicted the beasts he hunted and possibly worshipped. For his home, he preferred cave entrances or the shelter of a cliff overhang.

These stone-age artists' materials included red and yellow oxidised iron, powdered ochre, black charcoal and animal fats. They blew the powdered colour on to the walls of the caves through hollow bones or vegetable stalks basically the same technique as that used by aerosol-graffiti artists.

visit for the weirdly shaped stalagmites and stalactites and the panorama of the Vézère Valley.

Dordogne

The name **Dordogne** (www.dordogne-perigord-tourisme.fr) is given to a river, a *département* of France and to a larger surrounding area that is sometimes extended to the whole Périgord region. It has been popular with British and Dutch visitors for many years, and many British people have chosen to become permanent residents

The river itself flows through changing terrain, from its source in the Auvergne mountains through deep gorges to fertile lowlands and on to the sea near Bordeaux.

The landscape in the tour proposed below is dominated by the river, as it flows between limestone cliffs, meadows and woodland. The river is good for both fishing and canoeing, and if you haven't brought your own bike for exploring the back country, you can rent one at Sarlat.

Start at the confluence of the Vézère and Dordogne rivers, where the hilltop village of **Limeuil** affords a fine view of both valleys and their bridges meeting at right angles down below. Drive south away from the river to **Cadouin**, with its impressive 12th-century Cistercian **abbey**, a major Périgord Romanesque church with a wooden belfry on a remarkable split pyramidal cupola. The soberly designed church contrasts with the more decorative Gothic and Renaissance sculpture of the cloister.

Back on the river, perched above a 150-m (490-ft) deep ravine, is the fairytale castle of **Beynac-et-Cazenac**. The barons of Beynac lost it in turn to Richard the Lion-Heart and Simon de Montfort, Earl of Leicester, before turning it into a Renaissance palace. Across the river are Beynac's rival, **Castelnaud**, now housing a museum of medieval warfare, and the privately owned 15th-century castle of **Fayrac**, complete with restored drawbridge, battlements and 'pepperpot' towers.

The village of **La Roque-Gageac**, which seems almost to be glued to an overhanging cliff, is known as one of the most beautiful (and most-visited) spots in the country. Its renown is especially well deserved when the late-afternoon sun catches the houses' stone-tiled roofs. It's also an antiques-collector's paradise, being peppered with antiques shops.

To get a wonderful view of the whole stretch of river, and to stretch your legs in a beautiful park-like setting, climb up to the **Château de Marqueyssac** (www.marqueyssac.com; daily July–Aug 9am–8pm, Apr–June and Sept 10am–7pm, Feb–Mar and Oct–mid-Nov 10am–6pm, mid-Nov–Jan 2–5pm) and its impressive *jardins suspendus* (hanging gardens).

Sarlat

The capital of the Périgord Noir, **Sarlat** ⑫ is a lovely old town with a fine mix of architecture, bustling in high season but quiet in spring and autumn. The **Saturday market** is a joy, as are the narrow streets of the old town east of busy rue de la République. Look out for the Gothic and Renaissance houses on rues Fénelon and des Consuls (especially **Hôtel Plamon**) and for place du Peyrou's grand **Maison de la Boétie**, across from the cathedral. An open-air summer festival is held on place de la Liberté, the marketplace and a centre for cafés and shops.

Specialities of the region include truffles, wild mushrooms, foie gras and walnuts. Don't leave Sarlat without trying the *pommes sarladaises,* thin-sliced potatoes sautéed in goose fat with garlic and parsley.

Rocamadour

Since the 12th century, sightseers and religious pilgrims alike have been flocking to the spectacularly situated fortified town of **Rocamadour** ⑬, atop a cliff above the Alzou river (best appreciated from the village of L'Hospitalet across the valley). Founded on the tomb of a hermit, St-Amadour, which was believed to have mystic curative powers, Rocamadour attracted Henry II of England and a number of French kings after him.

The present-day mobs of tourists buzzing around the souvenir shops of the old town capture something of the medieval frenzy. Pilgrims would climb the 216 steps of the via Sancta on their knees to get to the shrines halfway up the cliffs. These include the **Chapelle Miraculeuse de Notre-Dame**, with its statue of the Black Virgin, and the 12th-century basilica. Higher up are a château and ramparts.

The great chasm *(gouffre)* of **Padirac**, 16km (10 miles) northeast of Rocamadour, is one of Périgord's most exciting natural wonders. Elevators take you 100m (328ft) down to a subterranean river for a spooky boat ride past gigantic stalactites and stalagmites, formed by the calcite residue and deposits of thousands of years of dripping water.

Château de Puymartin, another in a region thick with châteaux

THE ATLANTIC COAST

In contrast to the Mediterranean coast, the Atlantic offers wide open spaces, beaches with rolling waves and high dunes, and vast stretches of quiet pine forests. The wines and seafood are excellent and abundant, and there's plenty for children to do here too.

La Rochelle

One of the most handsome of France's ports, **La Rochelle** Ⓐ has always been innovative and today is known as *belle et rebelle* (beautiful and rebellious). It was one of the first communities in Europe to experiment with democracy, electing its first mayor in 1199, and was long a Protestant bastion in a Catholic country. More recently it has been a leader in urban planning, careful to preserve its quiet charm and dignity. La Rochelle was one of the first towns in France to introduce a pedestrian-only zone, and today rental bicycles (€1 per half hour) are available for visitors.

Surrounded by lively cafés, with an avenue of trees along one quay, the old harbour still serves the fishing fleet and small sailing boats. Its entrance is guarded by two 14th-century towers remaining from the town's fortifications. To the left, the **Tour St-Nicolas** served as a fortress and prison. At the foot of the **Tour de la Chaîne**, formerly a gunpowder storehouse, lies the huge chain once slung across to St-Nicolas to bar passage at night.

In the grand old lighthouse (and second prison), the **Tour de la Lanterne**, you will find prisoners' graffiti on the walls as you climb up to the balcony for a view over the city and the bay. The Gothic tower gate and belfry, Porte de la Grosse-Horloge, leads into the prosperous old merchant quarters with gracefully vaulted shopping arcades and 16th- and 17th-century houses. Don't miss the handsome Renaissance **Hôtel de Ville** (on

Bloody siege

In 1627 Cardinal Richelieu laid siege to the Huguenot stronghold of La Rochelle. When the siege finally ended, after 15 bloody months, only a mere 5,000 of the original 28,000 inhabitants were still alive.

La Rochelle, one of France's loveliest ports

rue des Merciers) with its Italian-style courtyard, staircase and belfry. Another elegant house is the double-gabled ex-hotel, now part of an international artists' residence, hidden away at the rear of a garden (11 rue des Augustins).

La Rochelle has several museums, among them the **Musée du Nouveau Monde** (10 rue Fleuriau; museedunouveaumonde.larochelle. fr; mid-June–mid Sept Mon, Wed–Sun 10am–6pm, Sat 2–6pm, rest of the year Mon, Wed–Sun 10.30am–12.30pm, 1.30–5.30pm, Sat 1.30–5.30pm), which explores the town's early trading links with the New World; the **Musée des Beaux-Arts** (28 rue Gargoulleau; museedesbeauxarts.laro- chelle.fr; temporarily closed for renovation), which includes paintings by Giordano and Corot; and the huge **Aquarium** (avenue du Lazaret). Children will enjoy the **Musée Maritime** (museemaritime.larochelle.fr; same hours) with exhibits housed in three ships.

Ile de Ré

With its gleaming white villas and smart little hotels, a sunny micro- climate, a network of cycle paths, beautiful pine-shaded beaches and succulent oysters and mussels, this cheerful island is a popular holiday resort, especially among sailors. Visit the **Phare des Baleines** (www. pharedesbaleines.com; daily Apr–June 10am–7pm, July–Aug 9.30am–9pm, Sept 10am–6.30pm, Oct–Mar 10.30am–5.30pm), a lighthouse at the western end of the island (257 steps to the view at the top). Boats to the Ile de Ré leave from La Rochelle's Vieux Port.

Bordeaux

Anyone interested in ships will no doubt head first for the great port of **Bordeaux** ⓰ to inspect the ocean-going freighters. Guided boat tours depart from the landing stage (Embarcadère Vedettes) of the vast esplanade des Quinconces.

Others may prefer to stay ashore in the cafés, shops and galleries around the **place de la Comédie**. The square is dominated by the **Grand Théâtre**, the jewel of Bordeaux's many 18th-century buildings. It is a neoclassical structure of twelve Corinthian columns, adorned with statues of Greek muses and goddesses. The majestic double staircase inside inspired Charles Garnier for his design of the Paris opera house.

Running along the redeveloped riverside are wide pedestrianised paths for walkers, skaters and cyclists (Bordeaux is a very skate-friendly city) and generously planted borders, Europe's largest water mirror (reflecting Place de la Bourse in all its glory) and also the Cité du Vin, the city's ultra-modern and gleaming cultural centre dedicated to wine. Just inland from there, the wonderful Bassins des Lumières is a digital art exhibition which shows huge immersive artworks that reflect in the water of the disused submarine base. Back on the other side of the river Garonne you get a taste of the other more progressive side to this historic city; Darwin is an ex-military barracks that has been re-imagined into an urban ecosystem with skatepark, sustainable shops, co-working space, cafés and an events stage too.

The old **quartier St-Pierre** around the church of the same name is a masterpiece of urban renewal. The once ill-famed slum has grown into a lively neighbourhood of art galleries and little shops, with an open-air market on place St-Pierre. On the beautifully renovated houses along rues Phillippart and Bahutiers, notice the grotesque masks and winged angels sculpted over the doorways. The dimensions of the gigantic Flamboyant Gothic **Cathédrale St-André** rival those of Notre-Dame de Paris, which is a mere 6m (20ft) longer and 4m (13ft) wider.

The **Musée des Beaux-Arts** (cours d'Albert; www.musba-bordeaux.fr; Wed–Mon 11am–6pm) includes works by Veronese, Perugino, Rubens and Van Dyck, as well as major paintings by Delacroix and Matisse. The **Musée d'Art Contemporain** (also known as CAPC, 7 rue Ferrère; www.capc-bordeaux.fr; Tue–Sun 11am–6pm, second Wed of the month until 8pm) has a collection of contemporary art.

St-Emilion

Just inland from Bordeaux and at the western end of the Dordogne Valley, St-Emilion is undoubtedly the most attractive of the Bordeaux wine villages, not least due to the golden-tinted stone of the medieval houses around its sleepy place du Marché. With two monasteries, St Emilion offers a wealth of religious architecture. Unique in Europe, the 1,000-year-old church known as the **Eglise Monolithe** was carved out of the solid rock on which the village is built. After wandering around the old ramparts and narrow streets, take a rest in the ivy-covered ruins of the 14th-century **Cloître des Cordeliers**.

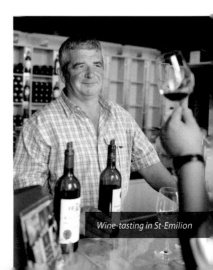

Wine-tasting in St-Emilion

The town gives its name to yet another wine district. Honoured by the English as the 'King of Wines', the quality has been supervised for eight centuries by red-robed jurors

Central Pyrenees landscape

in one of the town's many Gothic cloisters. The local Maison du Vin can give advice for your tour of the surrounding vineyards. Not far away is the superb Roman villa at Montcaret (near Lamothe-Ravel on the road to Bergerac).

THE PYRENEES

The second-highest mountain range in France, the **Pyrenees** form a natural border with Spain and are snowcapped year-round. Tourism in the high mountains is not as evident as in the Alps, although there is some downhill and cross-country skiing, and camping and hiking are popular in the unspoiled scenery of the **Parc National des Pyrénées**, where trails are well marked. Wildflowers cover the high pastures in spring and early summer, and the wildlife ranges from butterflies to bears. Tourist offices throughout the region can help with information on the park. **Andorra**, a principality high in the mountains and owned jointly by France and Spain, is a popular ski resort and centre for duty-free shopping. There is good hiking away from the busy towns, but it is a long, hard drive from the French side.

Biarritz

Lovers of nostalgia will appreciate the patina of faded grandeur of the elegant resort of **Biarritz** ⑥ where Queen Victoria once promenaded along the front, and Bismarck fell madly in love with the wife of a Russian ambassador. Known as the 'queen of beaches and the beach of kings', the town was made fashionable by Napoleon III and Empress Eugénie and became known as the site of elaborate – even wild – parties. Though it still has a thriving nightlife, the town is more sedate today and is a favourite of retirees and surfers. There are good beaches, 10 golf courses within a 20-km (12-mile) radius of the town, and ample opportunities for tennis, horse-riding and windsurfing.

At the aquarium of the **Musée de la Mer** (Rocher de la Vierge; www.aquariumbiarritz.com; daily July–Aug 9am–10pm, rest of the year 9.30am–7pm), you can see more than 150 species of fish and invertebrates from the Bay of Biscay, a seal pool (with daily feedings) and an underwater tunnel of sharks.

Pays Basque

The rural **Pays Basque** (or known in Basque as Euzkadi) stretches south into Spain along a coastal plain and through the Pyrenees. The mountain sides and valleys are dotted with gleaming white, gabled houses, set off by russet brown timbering. The French Basques – generally less separatist than their Spanish brethren – are nevertheless an independent people, proud of their cultural differences from the rest of France and of their obscure language, known as Euskara.

Basque

No connection between Basque and any other language has ever been proven. In France it is spoken by approximately 51,000 people. It is a complex language in many ways (the conjugation of verbs in particular) but it often lacks vocabulary for concepts and tools and borrows heavily from French and Spanish for such words.

Biarritz might be the best-known town in the Basque country, but **Bayonne** is the regional capital. The **Musée Basque** (Château-Neuf; www.musee-basque.com; Tue–Wed Fri–Sun 10am–6pm, Thu 1pm–8pm) provides a valuable introduction to the folklore of the region. Bayonne is a good town to visit on foot, with a pedestrian shopping area around the 13th-century cathedral, parks, ramparts and quays along the two rivers. The collection of the **Musée Bonnat-Helleu** (5 rue Jacques Laffitte; closed for restoration until 2025) includes paintings by Rubens, El Greco, Degas, Titian, Raphael and Watteau.

The pretty fishing village and artists' colony of **St-Jean-de-Luz** has a sheltered **harbour** with a sandy beach and lively cafés, galleries and boutiques. The town's great claim to fame is the wedding of Louis XIV to the Spanish Infanta María Teresa in 1660. The houses that lodged them, **Maison de Louis XIV** and **Maison de l'Infante**, still stand by the port. The austere facade of the 15th-century **Eglise St-Jean-Baptiste**, where the wedding was celebrated, doesn't prepare you for the characteristic Basque

The Pont Napoléon in the High Pyrenees is popular with bungee jumpers

interior: carved oak galleries to separate the various classes of worshippers on three sides of a single nave, with polychrome wooden vaulting and a three-tiered gilded-and-crimson Baroque altar.

Southeast of St-Jean-de-Luz is **Ascain**, with a village square surrounded by lovely 17th-century houses and a typical wooden-galleried church. A rack-and-pinion railway at Col de St-Ignace carries you 900m (2,950ft) up to the top of **La**

Cycling in this region is arduous

Rhune for an exhilarating view of the Atlantic Ocean and the western Pyrenees. In the pretty village of Ainhoa each sturdy-beamed whitewashed house painted with Basque inscriptions is of a different height and juts out at a different angle.

St-Jean-Pied-de-Port was the last stage before crossing into Spain on one of the main routes of pilgrimage to Santiago de Compostela – and you can still follow the pilgrims' path around the **ramparts**, up a stairway through Porte St-Jacques to the **ville haute** (upper town). Rustic red-sandstone houses line rue de la Citadelle, which leads to an old bridge across the Nive river with a pretty view of the town's Gothic church. For a panorama across the Nive Valley, climb up to the **citadel**, built by Louis XIV as a defence against a potential Spanish invasion.

Pau

Pau ⑰ is famous for its views of the Pyrenees and as the birthplace of Henri IV, in 1553. During the 19th century, Pau became something of a British colony. The British provided two mayors and left their mark with horseracing, fox hunting and the country's first golf club. Today,

Café life in Toulouse

the **Château de Pau**, restored in the 19th century and more Renaissance palace than fortress is an interesting museum of Gobelins tapestries and paraphernalia from the early life of the country's most popular king. Stroll along the terrace at the foot of the château, known as **boulevard des Pyrénées**, for the region's most spectacular view of the snowcapped peaks lining the southern horizon. On the balustrade along the edge of the boulevard are little notches, which, if aligned with the lightning rod of the tram factory below, will point to the major peaks.

The chief treasure of the town's **Musée des Beaux-Arts** (Wed–Mon 10am–noon, 2–6pm) is a fascinating painting by Degas, *The New Orleans Cotton Exchange*.

Toulouse

Centre of the national aerospace industry, with a vigorous local culture, the university city of **Toulouse** 68 has an infectious enthusiasm to it. The rose-brick old town – with its many Renaissance mansions built with the proceeds of the dye, textile and grain trades – is best seen on foot. At the heart is the huge 18th-century **Hôtel de Ville** (Capitole), fronted by an open space where an open-air market is held on Wednesday mornings.

The 11th-century **Basilique St-Sernin** is the largest Romanesque church in Europe and an undisputed masterpiece among French architecture. The **Eglise des Jacobins** (Tue–Sun 10am–6pm; free), burial place of the philosopher and theologian St Thomas Aquinas, is a Gothic fortress church, with a noble tower, elegant twin-columned **cloister**, and a remarkable interior of polychrome beauty (subtle dark reds, pink and buff).

Two examples of palatial townhouses, funded by the local pastel trade, are the **Hôtel d'Assézat** (place d'Assézat), now home to the Fondation Bemberg art gallery (www.fondation-bemberg.fr; Tue–Sun 10am–12.30pm, 1.30–6pm) which includes 36 works by Bonnard, and the **Hôtel de Bernuy** (1 rue Gambetta).

La Cité de l'Espace (exit 17 or 18 from the ring road; *métro* Marengo; www.cite espace.com; daily; hours vary, check website) is a huge space complex, with a planetarium and a park laid out like the solar system, dominated by a replica of the Ariane rocket in whose control room you can prepare for take-off and watch the deployment of a satellite. At 35 allées Jules Guesde, Muséum de Toulouse (www.museum.toulouse.fr; Tue–Sun 10am–6pm) houses an impressive natural history collection.

Albi

This serene and cheerful town on the river Tarn – built, like Toulouse, with red brick is known as *Albi la Rouge*.

In the 13th-century bishop's residence, the Palais de la Berbie, the **Musée Toulouse-Lautrec** (musee-toulouse-lautrec.com; daily June–Sept 10am–6pm, rest of the year Tue–Sun 10am–12.30pm, 2–6pm) honours the painter born in Albi in 1864 and houses the country's largest collection of his works and sketchbooks.

A walk along the banks of the river below the museum provides good views of the 11th-century bridge and the red-brick mills that used the flow of water to power a variety of industries.

The **Gorges du Tarn**, 100km (60 miles) to the east of Albi are well worth a detour. Near the town of Le Rozier, the river narrows to just a few metres wide and is towered over by cliffs rising to about 300m (1,000ft).

LANGUEDOC-ROUSSILLON

The coast of Languedoc-Roussillon offers lovely fishing ports as well as a string of sparkling new resorts, which are distinguished by their golden

Medieval Carcassonne and its surrounding vineyards

beaches and modern architecture. Inland, the towns of Carcassonne and Toulouse offer a contrast between the area's old roots and its forward-looking aspirations.

Carcassonne

The restored medieval town of **Carcassonne 69** will delight everyone who likes fairy-tale castles. It has served as a fortress for the Gallo-Romans, the Visigoths, Franks and medieval French (you can see the layers of their masonry in the ramparts). It is a very popular tourist destination and full of souvenir shops; try to beat the crowds early in the day and return in the evening.

Carcassonne can be disappointing at first sight; the best overall view is from the *autoroute*, and the town is perhaps most impressive when illuminated at night. Most people park on the east side of the old town (*la Cité*) and walk over the drawbridge of the **Porte Narbonnaise**. But you'll get a much better feel for the medieval atmosphere of a fortified town, with its ramparts and lookout towers, if you park on the western side, by the church of St-Gimer, and walk up around the old **Château Comtal**.

Although much of Carcassonne is authentic, Viollet-le-Duc, the architect who masterminded the restoration, took liberties where he lacked the original plans. An example of this is the Romanesque-Gothic **Basilique St-Nazaire**, which he thought was originally part of the fortifications and so blithely added battlements to the west façade. In the choir, you can see fine 13th- and 14th-century sculptures and stained-glass windows.

Perpignan

Though its outskirts may be a bit scruffy, **Perpignan ⓖ** is well worth a visit. The city has a Spanish feel and in fact was only ceded to France in 1659 after being part of the Catalan province of the Spanish kingdom of Aragon. From the 10th to the 17th centuries it was the mainland capital of the kings of Mallorca and it is possible to visit the late 13th-century **Palais des Rois de Majorque** (rue des Archers; daily July–Aug 9.30am–6.30pm, Apr–May and Sept–Oct 10am–6pm, Nov–Mar 10am 5pm). Perpignan is heavily steeped in Catalan culture and character reflected in both language and cuisine. More on this subject can be found at **Casa Pairal** (La Castillet Place de Verdun; daily June–Sept 10.30am–6pm, rest of the year Tue–Sun 11am–5.30pm).

Béziers and the Golfe du Lion

Leaving Perpignan, head north for Béziers. Our route will then take you through the vineyards and beaches of Hércault and north to Montpellier.

Béziers ⓗ is a busy but compact city, with a delightful shady central promenade – lined with cafés and restaurants – called the **Allées Paul Riquet**, named after the engineer of the Canal du Midi. Among the sights in Béziers are the ancient **Eglise St-Jacques** and **Eglise Ste-Madeleine**, the 19th-century **Halles** (covered market) and the massive **Cathédrale St-Nazaire**, from which there is a good view over the river valley. The Canal du Midi crosses the Orb river on its *pont canal* at Béziers.

For a bit of a detour turn west from Béziers on the D612 and after 24km (miles) turn left for the ancient port of **Agde**, founded by the Greeks more than 25 centuries ago. Agde presents a sombre face – many of its buildings were constructed from the local volcanic basalt, including the 12th-century **Cathédrale St-Etienne** – but the narrow streets on the hill leading up to the market square are cheerful and friendly.

For a total change of pace, continue to **Cap d'Agde**. Only minutes from Agde itself, this is a modern resort built in traditional Languedoc style. Its many quays bristle with luxury yachts and there are shops, cafés and restaurants to suit every taste. It also features a large nudist enclave (Port Nature) – the largest nudist colony in Europe, complete with *naturiste* shopping mall and nightclubs.

From Agde, take the D51 to **Marseillan**, another ancient port, initially settled by the Phoenicians. The covered market, built in volcanic stone from Agde with a timber frame, dates back to the 17th century. The harbour, with views across the bay towards Sète, is a pleasant walk from the middle of town. Take time to sit at a café and watch the fishing boats mix with the tourists in yachts and narrowboats headed for the Canal du Midi. Also in the harbour are the wineries at **Chais Noilly Prat**, where you can view how the famous vermouth is made, and a small château that was once the home of the Noilly Prat family (now a restaurant).

From Marseillan, our route takes you down to Marseillan-Plage and up the D612 along more than 7km (4 miles) of flat, sandy beach – at weekends in August the crowds and numbers of cars can make this a slow trip – to **Sète**.

Back on the main road north of Béziers is the little town of **Pézenas**, home to royal governors of the region in the 16th and 17th centuries and once called the 'Versailles of the south'. You can easily spend a couple of hours strolling around the town looking at the fine mansions (50 or more) and the narrow streets of the medieval Jewish **ghetto**. A brochure from the tourist office gives a suggested walking tour and the sights are well marked. Keep your eyes open for Renaissance details, grand doorways and views into lovely courtyards. Among the buildings to watch for are the **Hôtel des Barons de Lacoste** (8 rue Francois-Oustrin) and the **Maison des Pauvres** (12 rue Alfred Sabatier). The **Musée de Vulliod-St-Germain** (3 rue Albert-Paul Alliès, mid-April–Sept

Tue–Wed, Fri–Sat 10am–noon, 3–7pm, Sun 3–7pm, mid-Feb–Apr and Oct–mid-Nov Tue–Wed, Fri–Sat10am–12.15pm, 2–5pm) has collections of furniture, faïence and tapestries, as well as memorabilia of the time the playwright Molière spent in the town with his troupe of actors.

Continue on the D613, passing through **Montagnac**, site of an interesting church from the 13th century. Carry on through Méze and soon you will get a good view over the Bassin de Thau and the oyster and mussel beds near **Bouzigues**. Continue on to **Sète** ⑫. The town is one of the Mediterranean's biggest industrial and fishing ports, but at its heart is an old town built over a network of canals and bridges with shops selling ships' lamps and propellers. It is an ideal place for landlubbers fond of seafood, and most of its restaurants can be found along the Grand Canal, with its funky Italianate houses painted in dusty shades of rose pink, pistachio and Camargue blue. Quayside restaurants serve huge platters of *fruits de mer* – mussels, oysters, sea snails – all delivered straight off the boat. From Sète, cruise boats take passengers round the Bassin de Thau and its oyster beds, and promise fishing trips and alfresco *sardines grillées*.

Sète is home to the **Centre Régional d'Art Contemporain** (CRAC; 29 quai Aspirant Herber; crac.laregion.fr; Mon, Wed–Fri 12.30–7pm, Sat–Sun 2–7pm). Above the town is the Cimetière Marin, on Mont St-Clair, where Sète's most famous son, poet Paul Valéry, is buried. (Other luminaries from Sète include singer Georges Brassens.) Nearby is the refurbished museum, the **Museé Paul Valéry** (rue François Resnoyes; museepaulvalery-sete.fr; daily

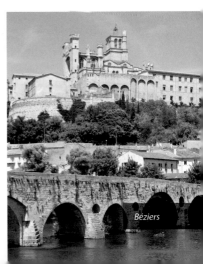

Béziers

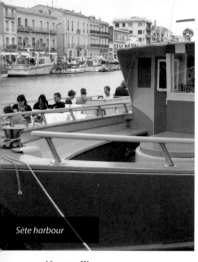

Sète harbour

Tue–Sun 10am–6pm). Also up here is the open-air Théâtre de la Mer, or Théâtre Jean-Vilar, in a citadel built by Vauban. From Mont St-Clair there are fine views over the oyster beds of the Bassin de Thau, and to the south, a long stretch of undeveloped, sandy beach. Boisterous water-jousting tournaments, a medieval throwback, are a popular spectator sport in Sète. From here take the D612 to Montpellier.

Montpellier

Montpellier ⑦ is a good base for visits both south into Languedoc-Roussillon and east into the Camargue and Provence. It's a lively university town, at the Mediterranean end of the Southwest, the two centres of city life are situated around the broad **place de la Comédie** and **place Jean-Jaurès**. During the day, a market of fresh fruit and meat, clothes and jewellery bustles until early afternoon. Once cleared, the square is filled with tables and chairs from the surrounding cafés. In the evening, it's a popular meeting place for students and well-heeled locals.

For a quieter glass of wine or cup of coffee, try the pretty **place du Marché-aux-Fleurs**, shaded by plane trees around a Henry Moore sculpture. And on rues des Trésoriers de France and des Trésoriers de la Bourse, you'll discover handsome 17th- and 18th-century **mansions** with imposing stairways in the inner courtyards. The **Musée Fabre** (boulevard Sarrail; museefabre.montpellier3m.fr; Tue–Sun 10am–6pm) has an outstanding art collection, including important paintings by Gustave Courbet, Eugène Delacroix, Matisse and Rubens.

For many, the most enchanting spot in town is the late-17th-century

promenade du Peyrou – spacious classical gardens with a triumphal arch, an equestrian statue of Louis XIV and, on a mound at the far end, a hexagonal *château d'eau* that looks more like a temple than a water tower and provides a fine view south to the Mediterranean and north to the Cévennes mountains.

For a refreshing look at modern urban development, visit the neo-classical **Antigone** quarter, on the opposite side of place de la Comédie from the old town.

Nîmes

The Emperor Augustus made a gift of **Nîmes** ⑦ (56km/35 miles north of Montpellier) to the veterans of his victory over Antony and Cleopatra in Egypt, commemorated to this day in the town's coat of arms with the chained crocodile of the Nile. The grand Roman **amphitheatre** was built for gladiator battles and held more than 20,000 spectators. Today it is the site of a variety of events including traditional bullfighting (in which the bull is killed) and Provençal-style bullfighting (in which it isn't).

The more peaceful Greek-style temple known as the **Maison Carrée**, dating from the 1st century BC, and considered to be the best-preserved Roman example still standing. Opposite in an ultramodern building, the **Carré d'Art** (www.carreartmusee.com; Tue–Fri 10am–6pm, Sat–Sun 10am–6.30pm) exhibits modern art. The rooftop restaurant offers a good view over the town. The Musée de la Romanité (museedelaromanite.fr; Sun–Mon 10am–7pm, Nov–Mar closes at 6pm) opened in 2018) opposite the Arena of Nîmes, and features an interactive take on the town's Roman history.

The **Jardin de la Fontaine** – a pretty, tree-shaded 18th-century park on the slopes of Mont Cavalier at the northwest edge of the town – offers a refreshing respite from the summer heat and a good view of the surrounding mountains. The park is built around the spring of Nemausus, which gave the town its name; it includes a ruined temple attributed to the hunting goddess Diana, and the octagonal **Tour Magne**, once part of the Roman walls.

Kayaking in Brantôme, Dordogne

THINGS TO DO

In addition to its historical attractions and fine opportunities for wining and dining, France has much to offer the visitor in terms of sporting opportunities, shopping, nightlife and festivals, all of which are covered in this chapter.

SPORTS

The diversity of climate and geography across the country means that most sports are available in France. In recent years the French have increasingly become devotees of outdoor sports such as running, hiking, biking, surfing and windsurfing. Regional tourist offices will be able to advise on local opportunities available.

OUTDOOR PURSUITS

For **runners**, the Paris marathon is in spring, but if you want to combine exercise with fun, good food and wine, try the Marathon du Médoc, a spirited three-day event held in September.

There are few better sports than **hiking** for making the most of the French countryside. Tourist offices will be able to suggest itineraries, many of them marked in red or blue on trees or lampposts along the trail. Some of these itineraries are guided tours for botany or geology enthusiasts. Experienced hikers can try the challenging hikes called *grandes randonnées* through the Alps, the Pyrénées and the Lubéron mountains of Provence (for details, contact the Fédération Française de Randonnées Pédestres, 64 rue de Dessous des Berges, 75013 Paris; tel: 01 44 89 93 90; www.ffrandonnee.fr).

Possibilities to play **tennis** are endless but it may not be easy to rent equipment. Hard surface courts can be found in municipal parks or attached to hotels. The latter can often help you with temporary membership to private clubs.

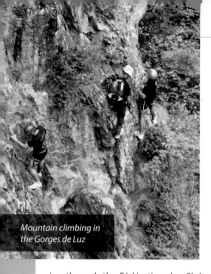

Mountain climbing in the Gorges de Luz

Bring your **golf** club membership card for easier access to the best courses in the major seaside resorts – Le Touquet, Dinard, Deauville, La Baule, Biarritz, and Mandelieu (Cannes). Around Paris, world-class courses are to be found at Fontainebleau, Chantilly, St-Cloud and St-Nom-la-Bretèche.

WINTER ACTIVITIES

Mountaineering novices can obtain advice and training through the Fédération des Clubs Alpins Français (24 avenue de Laumière, 75019 Paris, www.ffcam.fr); the club's local branches in the resort towns of the Alps and the Pyrénées dispense advice and information to experts and novices alike.

Generally speaking, the Alps are best for **downhill skiing** and the Pyrénées for **cross-country** *(ski de fond)*. For the latter, you might consider Corsica. In France, only a small number of established ski resorts, such as Megève and Val d'Isère, have some tradition and a village life to supplement the activity on the slopes. These are best for families who want first-class ski schools for kids and other beginners. Experienced skiers tend to head for specialised winter-sports *stations* with excellent facilities, high-tech equipment, the most challenging *pistes* and frenetic nightlife but less character, such as Les Arcs, Tignes, La Plagne and Avoriaz. Wherever you go for your skiing, if you're not travelling with children, try to avoid the busy school holidays.

Whether your principal means of transport is car, train or even boat, **cycling** is ideal for excursions. You can rent bicycles at many railway stations across the country, and bicycles can be carried free on selected trains. Cycling is a pleasant way to tour the vineyards of Champagne, Burgundy or Alsace.

Horse riding is a delight in the forests of the Ile-de-France as well as further afield in Brittany or in the area around Pau in the Pyrenees. And there are plenty of possibilities for good horse riding in other parts of the country, too. For information about a range of riding holidays dotted throughout France, with accommodation and meals included, contact the Fédération Française d'Equitation on +33 02 54 94 46 00, or visit www.ffe.com.

BOULES

Perched on a borderline between sport and folklore, the grand Provençal game of *boules*, or *pétanque*, is the perfect expression of regional character. At a distance, all seems tranquil in the sandy village square, where half a dozen or more men lob heavy metal balls along a shady avenue of plane trees. But get closer and you'll discover a ferocious combat, in which apparent good humour barely conceals high passions.

The object of the game is to get the maximum number of balls as close as possible to a little wooden jack, called the *cochonnet* (literally piglet). Good *boules* acquire the patina of medieval cannonballs. Players form teams of two (*doublettes*), three (*triplettes*) or four (*quadrettes*). They may be meticulous *pointeurs*, aiming close to the jack, or debonair *tireurs*, bombing the opponent's ball out of the way. The most important piece of equipment is a piece of string, to determine the distance between the *boules* and the cochonnet and who pays for the next round of pastis.

Boules and *pétanque* are often used interchangeably, but there is a difference between them. *Pétanque* is from 'Pied' for feet and 'tanque' is regional dialect for together or tangled, inferring that you cannot move your feet. This is the form most commonly played now, although many French players simply call it *jeu de boules*.

WATER SPORTS

Swimming may be most glamorous on the Côte d'Azur, but you'll find the Brittany and smaller Normandy resorts much less crowded. The pollution count is displayed at local town halls. Watch out for the occasional stinging jellyfish *(méduse)* in the Mediterranean; and be careful when swimming at the more secluded Atlantic beaches where there are no lifeguards on regular duty. Many French municipalities have excellent Olympic-size pools, and more and more hotels are installing them, too. Expect a certain amount of near-nudity on beaches anywhere.

You can rent *planches à voile* for **wind surfing** in the major resorts. Straight surfing is an Atlantic sport, best at Biarritz.

Canoeing and kayaking are both popular, particularly in Périgord. For details of nationwide facilities, contact the Fédération Française de Canoë-Kayak, Stade Nautique Olympique d'Ile-de-France, Route de Torcy, Vaires sur Marne, tel: 01 45 11 08 50, www.ffck.org.

Hang gliding and **paragliding** are both becoming increasingly popular in France. Contact the Fédération Française de Vol Libre, 1 place du Général Goiran, Nice, tel: 04 97 03 82 82, www.ffvl.fr.

Cycling in Alsace

Fish for trout and pike in the Annecy and Le Bourget lakes; trout, carp, shad, and bream in the Burgundy rivers, the Dordogne and tributaries of the Loire. For regional fishing information, contact Atout France, tel: 01 42 96 70 00, www.atout-france.fr. Deep-sea expeditions are often advertised at the port, especially in Brittany and at La Rochelle.

SPECTATOR SPORTS

Cycle racing remains extremely popular. The Tour de France in July is a major national event, with each stage of the race, which is at its most strenuous and exciting in the Alps or Pyrenees, resembling a local festival.

Pelote is a Basque speciality. It is roughly along the lines of squash, but played with a leather-bound ball that is hurled at the wall with an elongated basket-glove known as a *chistera*.

> ## Pedalling pedigree
>
> Although the Tour de France is the most famous cycle race, the oldest is the Paris–Brest, established in 1891. Now an amateur event, held every four years, the Paris–Brest requires riders to complete the 1,200km-route in less than 90 hours. In true French style, a wheel-shaped cake is named after the event.

The Roman amphitheatres of Arles and Nîmes make dramatic settings for the annual summer **bullfights.**

A major **tennis** tournament is held in Monte-Carlo in May that's an important warm-up for Paris's French Open at Roland-Garros in June, just before Wimbledon. See if your hotel concierge can get you tickets.

In **motor racing,** the most spectacular events, in late May or early June, are the Grand Prix at Monaco and the 24-hour race at Le Mans (a day trip from the Loire Valley or Normandy).

In Paris, **horse racing** enthusiasts go to Auteuil for the steeplechase and Longchamp for flat racing, June and early October being the months for the great classics. Chantilly (in June) and Deauville (in August) claim equally prestigious events.

ENTERTAINMENT

While Paris is still without a doubt the undisputed major focus for theatre, classical concerts, ballet, and opera, you'll find plenty going on in the provinces, particularly in the summer when even the tiniest Provençal or

Périgord village stages some kind of arts festival. A programme listing all major festivals and *fêtes* throughout the country is published annually and is available from French Government Tourist Offices across the country.

For details of what's on in the capital, consult listings magazine *L'Officiel des Spectacles* (www.offi.fr). It appears every Wednesday with full details of cultural events and venues in and around the city.

CLASSICAL MUSIC, OPERA AND BALLET

Paris continues to offer many fine concerts at its first-class venues, including the Opéra Bastille, the glamorous Théâtre des Champs-Elysées, the Théâtre du Châtelet, the Opéra Comique, the Philharmonie de Paris and the Salle Pléyel. The palatial Opéra de Paris-Garnier now specialises in ballet, while opera is performed at the Opéra Bastille. Innovative music can be found at the Cité de la Musique, which is adjacent to the Philharmonie de Paris. Historic churches also host many performances, particularly of Baroque and choral music. There are usually free organ concerts at the Madeleine, Notre-Dame and St-Eustache on Sunday in the afternoon or early evening.

Unfortunately, the number of regular concerts and performances dwindles in Paris in the summer. Tourists should be aware of festivals such as the Paris Quartier d'Eté, which stages performances around the town, often in open-air settings. Outside Paris, the major cities have first-class orchestras and the various summer

Chanson

With their roots in nightclubs and the music hall, French chansonniers seem to exemplify the chic yet sleazy Parisian nightlife of the popular imagination. Singers such as Juliette Gréco, Charles Aznavour, Yves Montand, Maurice Chevalier, Charles Trénet and, above all, Edith Piaf, projected an enduring image of the fragile but tough sentimentalist, whose songs veer between angst and frivolity.

festivals bring top international performers.

THEATRE

In Paris, the Comédie-Française (rue de Richelieu) is the high temple of French classical drama, showing works by Molière, Racine and Corneille. On the Left Bank, the Odéon – Théâtre de l'Europe (place de l'Odéon) puts on international productions, with prestigious guest companies performing in English, German and Italian.

Miles Davis statue in front of the Negresco hotel in Nice

You'll find contemporary and repertory theatre at the Théâtre National de la Colline and Théâtre National de Chaillot and at a number of smaller privately run theatres. The most important centres of provincial theatre include Nancy, Strasbourg, Toulouse, Lyon, Avignon and Montpellier.

JAZZ

The French take their jazz seriously. Paris has many clubs, and in the summer the action is on the Côte d'Azur. Of the Paris clubs, the New Morning (rue des Petites-Ecuries; www.newmorning.com) attracts major American and European musicians. Le Caveau de la Huchette (5 rue de la Huchette; www.caveaudelahuchette.fr) is known for big band sounds and jive; Au Duc des Lombards (42 rue des Lombards; www.ducdeslombards.com) offers a wide range and attracts American soloists. You can hear traditional and fusion jazz at the Le Sunset-Sunside (60 rue des Lombards; www.sunset-sunside.com). Other popular haunts include Le Baiser Salé (58 rue des Lombards, Le Baiser Salé; www.lebaisersale.com) and the Jazz Club Étoile (81 boulevard Gouvion St-Cyr; www.jazzclub-paris.com).

Avignon is famous for its annual theatre festival

ROCK

In Paris, concerts are held at the Zénith (in La Villette, *métro* Porte de Pantin; le-zenith.com) and the Olympia (28 boulevard des Capucines; www.olympia hall.com). La Maroquinerie (23 rue Boyer; www.lamaroquine rie.fr) is another more intimate venue. June 21 is the date for the *Fête de la musique* all over France, when bands perform all night long in the major cities.

CLUBBING

Clubs go in and out of fashion as fast as the music that's played in them; check the listings magazines for up-to-date information. The action doesn't usually start until well after midnight and getting home can be a challenge; plan to take a taxi unless you're lucky enough to be only a walk away. The expensive Paris clubs are located on the Champs-Elysées, notably on rue de Ponthieu and avenue Matignon, while the younger crowd haunt eardrum-busters around Les Halles. At the coastal resorts, the expensive discos are often attached to casinos and big hotels.

CINEMA

Not even Los Angeles or New York can match the French capital's average of 300 different films showing each week in over 100 cinemas. Practically all of them are available in at least one cinema in 'VO', an undubbed version with French subtitles. Study the weekly entertainment guides or *L'Officiel du Spectacle,* especially for the obscure gems offered by the Frank Gehry-designed *cinémathèque* (at 51 rue de Bercy; metro Cour St-Emilion; www.cinematheque.fr). Don't be intimidated by the queues; you nearly always get in.

SHOPPING

Since the 1980s, most major towns in France have made the decision to keep town centres for small boutiques and individual shops. Many of these areas are pedestrianised and very attractive (although beware – some cars ignore the *voie piétonne* signs). The large supermarkets, hypermarkets, furniture stores and do-it-yourself outlets collect on the outskirts of town, mostly designated as Centres Commercials. These centres, although aesthetically unappealing, are fine for bulk shopping for self-catering or for finding a selection of reasonably priced wine to take home. But for gifts and general window-shopping the town centres are far more interesting. It is here that you will find the individual souvenirs with a particularly local flavour, alongside the beautifully dressed windows of delicatessens and patisseries. Markets are also a good source of handmade regional goods.

SHOPPING BY AREA

The different regions of France are famous for particular products, for example Breton lace, Limoges porcelain, Provençal fabrics, perfume from Grasse, to name but a few. Paris, naturally, has an exceptional range of shops from the fashion houses in the 8th arrondissement, particularly around the

FRENCH FILM

The moving image was invented in France by the Lumière brothers, who made their first film in 1855. Generations of directors, from Jean Cocteau, Louis Malle and François Truffaut to Jean-Luc Besson and Mathieu Kassovitz, have been beguiled by the photogenic and romantic qualities of the French capital. After World War II, the city was seen as iconic in American films such as *Funny Face* and *An American in Paris*. Although now portrayed in a range of lights, the city is often shown as the home to troubled or oddball characters, whether in the tragic *Les Amants du Pont-Neuf*, the dark 1980s' *Subway*, the gritty *La Haine*, or the nostalgic, sugary-sweet *Amélie*.

Brocantes and the marchés aux puces are full of bargains

Faubourg St-Honoré, to the more affordable, but still chic department stores (grands magasins), such as Galeries Lafayette and Printemps (which has one of the largest perfume departments in the world), both of which are on boulevard Haussmann. The capital, as with many cities around France, is developing a good reputation for vintage and pre-loved clothing stores and Printemps has opened a whole floor dedicated to sustainable fashion pop-ups called 7eme Ciel (Seventh Heaven).

Les Trois Quartiers shopping arcade at the Madeleine in the 8th arrondissement, and the once slightly down-at-heel Les Halles, revamped and reopened in 2016, are also worth a visit. The Marais is a focus for youthful fashion boutiques and quirky gift shops.

OPENING HOURS

Food shops, especially bakers, tend to open early; boutiques and department stores open from 9am, but sometimes not until 10am. In most town centres, just about everything closes from noon until 2.30 or 3pm, but in Paris and other major tourist areas, some shops stay open. Most shops close in the evening at 7pm. Out of town and in areas frequented by tourists, hypermarkets are usually open all day until 8 or 9pm; in more remote areas they close for lunch and often shut at 7pm. Most shops are closed Monday mornings and a considerable number shut all day on Monday.

MARKET SHOPPING

The heart of every French town is its market, and shopping for fresh produce there is one of the real pleasures of holidaying in France. The markets usually start early in the morning and close at midday, although some bigger ones are open in the afternoon too. The French themselves usually visit early to get the best of the produce. Markets are a riot of colour and bustle; the best have all kinds of stalls from flowers to domestic animals (do not be deceived – these are for the pot). Local cheeses, honey, wine, pâté and other specialities are often offered for tasting to encourage browsers to buy.

Antiques or second-hand *(brocante)* markets are found all around the provinces, as well as flea markets (marchés aux puces), which are fun to look around – you may even find a genuine bargain antique amongst all the old junk. The most famous of these, indeed the biggest flea market in the world, is Les Puces de St-Ouen at Porte de Clignancourt in Paris, open Saturday to Monday 9am–6pm. There are also *vide greniers*, which are the equivalent of car boot sales.

Look out for special fairs held all over the country at various times throughout the year, such as harvest times; check with the local tourist office for details.

BUYING DIRECT

Around the country, you may be tempted by all the signs you see along the road for *dégustations* (tastings). Many wine producers and farmers will invite you to try their wines and other produce with an eye to selling you a case, or maybe a few jars of pâté. This is a good way to try before you buy and sometimes includes a visit to a wine cellar. Farm produce can be more expensive to buy this way than in the supermarkets – but do not forget that it is home-produced and not factory-processed, and it will be a lot fresher.

Visitors leaving France by car will probably find that stocking up at a *hypermarché* is the most economical choice. If you're flying out of the country, then you will find better bargains in the local supermarket than in the airport duty-free shops.

TAX

If you are a visitor from outside the European Union (EU), you can get a refund of the value-added tax (TVA – at time of writing 20 percent) on purchases amounting to €175 or more at any single store (displaying the tax free shopping sign) in one day. In most cases the refund is reduced by a small administration fee.

When you're making the purchase, ask for a tax-refund form. Present this to customs when you're leaving the EU. Show your purchases, receipts and passport and have the form stamped and then go to the Refund Office in the airport or mail the form back in the envelope provided and have it put back on your credit card.

Curio for sale in a brocante in Normandy

FESTIVALS AND EVENTS

This is a far-from-exhaustive list of both traditional and new cultural festivals. Visit www.culture.fr for more details.

January: Gérardmer (Vosges), science-fiction film festival; Champagne and Burgundy, village processions for wine-growers' patron St Vincent; Lyon, World Pastry Cup.

February: (or early March) Nice Mardi Gras carnival.

March: Paris Book Fair; Paris Documentary Film Festival.

April: Bourges, rock music; Arles, Easter bullfights in Roman amphitheatre; Paris Marathon.

May: Cannes, International Film Festival; Saint-Tropez, 'Bravade' religious procession; Stes-Maries-de-la Mer, Gypsy pilgrimage; Honfleur, Whitsuntide Fête des Marins (May/June); Nîmes, Whitsuntide bullfights in amphitheatre (May/June).

June: Strasbourg, classical music; Le Mans 24 Hour Race; Montpellier, music, opera, and dance, Tour de France (June/July).

July: Avignon, international theatre, music, opera, dance, and cinema; Aix-en-Provence, opera; Aix-en-Provence, jazz; Arles, photography seminars, exhibitions, and audiovisual shows in amphitheatre; Cluny, classical music; Juan-les-Pins, jazz festival; Orange, opera in the amphitheatre; Nice, jazz; Bayonne, folk festival; La Rochelle, Francofolies (music festival); Colmar, wine fair.

August: Annecy, fireworks by the lake; Chartres, organ recitals in cathedral (July/Aug), Assumption Day procession and Mass; Le Touquet, jazz and contemporary music; Dijon, wine festival; Prades, Festival Pablo Casals (chamber music).

September: Lyon, Dance Biennale (biennial, odd years only); Deauville, American film festival; Paris, Festival d'Automne (music and theatre; till December); Mont-Saint-Michel, procession and Mass for St Michael; Amiens Jazz Festival.

October: Dijon, sacred music; Nancy, jazz; Perpignan, jazz.

November: Burgundy (Beaunes, Nuits-Saint-Georges, Meursault, and Chablis), wine festivals; Dijon, gastronomy fair; Cannes, dance festival (biennial, odd years only).

December: Les Baux-de-Provence, Christmas Eve Fête des Bergers (shepherds) and Midnight Mass; Strasbourg and Alsatian villages, Christmas markets.

FOOD AND DRINK

Food plays a major role in life in France, and the French take eating very seriously, even if they lapse into fast food occasionally. Food in general is a favourite topic of conversation, and new restaurants are widely discussed. As the playwright Jean Anouilh once said, 'Everything ends this way in France – everything. Weddings, christenings, duels, burials, swindlings, diplomatic affairs – everything is a pretext for a good dinner.'

WHERE TO EAT

In the big cities, you'll have a wide choice: gourmet restaurants (relatively expensive); large family-style *brasseries* or more intimate bistros (more moderately priced); cafés or wine bars (for a light lunch or snack); and *crêperies* and street stalls offering slices of pizza, kebabs and Chinese and Japanese fare.

Pretty mosaic signage

Part of the fun is choosing where to eat. Priced menus are posted outside restaurants, making your taste buds tingle well in advance of the meal itself. Note that cafés list their prices prominently (a legal requirement), and that the same drink will be cheaper if you stand at the counter than if you sit at a table. Stroll around and make a reservation when you've made your choice. Sometimes menus stay the same for a long time, although increasing fondness for seasonal produce and cooking has

Parisian waiters

meant more frequent changes to menus. Specials are often simply listed on the menu as the *entrée du jour* or *plat du jour;* you will have to ask what it is.

Expect a full lunch to last a couple of hours, and an evening meal even longer. If you're in a hurry, choose a *brasserie* or *bistro* and let the person serving you know that you can't stay long.

MENU CHOICES

The typical 'continental' **breakfast** *(petit déjeuner)* is still croissant, brioche or bread and butter with coffee, tea or hot chocolate. Increasingly, orange juice is offered as an extra, but you must insist on *orange pressée* if you want it freshly squeezed. Big hotels offer English- and American-style breakfasts, but starting the day at the corner café will feel more authentic.

Traditionally, the French lunch *(déjeuner)* is as important as the evening meal, although this is becoming less so in Paris and the other major cities. A good alternative is a salad, omelette or a cheese, ham or pâté sandwich made in a long baguette.

Café lifestyle

In the provinces the **evening meal** *(dîner)* is served at 8 or 8.30pm, as opposed to 8.30 or 9pm in Paris and such favourite Parisian resorts as Deauville, St-Tropez or Cannes. The French are more relaxed than you may expect about dressing for dinner – a jacket is expected at smart places, but only a few insist on a tie.

The fixed-price *menu* – also called *table d'hôte, prix fixe,* or *menu fixe* – consisting of appetiser, main course and dessert is often the best value, particularly in the expensive establishments, where you get an introduction to the restaurant's specialities without paying the high *à la carte* prices. There may be as many as four or five choices of fixed-price *menus,* with differing numbers of courses. A *formule* usually means a special deal where you can choose either an appetiser and main course or a main course and dessert and may include a small carafe of wine.

Don't be surprised if you choose a more expensive menu and it is extended by the presentation of unexpected little treats or *amuse bouches* aimed to awaken, tease or cleanse the palate.

For reasonably priced wine, try the house *(réserve de la maison),* which is often served in carafes *(pichets)* by the quarter *(quart)* or half *(demi)* litre. Check the prices of apéritifs, bottled water, coffee and soft drinks before ordering, as these can add up.

WHAT TO EAT

Although the character of the cuisine varies from region to region, there are some basic dishes that you'll find throughout the country. Don't hesitate to ask – a name on a local menu may mean nothing to a visitor and your waiter will be glad to explain.

Typical **first courses** *(entrées* or *hors d'oeuvres)* range from simple *crudités* (raw vegetables) and *charcuterie* (cold meats) to soups and more elaborate seafood and egg dishes.

Most of the big cities get their fish fresh every day except Monday. Trout *(truite)* is delicious *au bleu* (poached absolutely fresh), *meunière* (sautéed in butter) or *aux amandes* (sautéed with almonds). At their best, *quenelles de brochet* (pike dumplings) are light and airy. Sole and turbot take on a new meaning when served with *sauce hollandaise,* a wonderful blend of egg yolks, butter and lemon juice.

Meat in France is generally cooked rarer than in other countries. You will be consulted how you want steaks and various cuts of lamb and duck cooked. Extra-rare is *bleu,* rare *saignant,* medium *à point,* and well done *bien cuit* (and frowned upon).

Steaks *(entrecôte* or *tournedos)* are often served with a wine sauce *(marchand de vin),* with shallots *(échalotes)* or with a rich sauce based on bone marrow *(à la moelle).* Roast leg of lamb *(gigot d'agneau)* is normally served pink *(rose).*

While each region tends to promote its own specialities, the most famous **cheeses** are available everywhere: the blue *Roquefort,* soft white crusted *Camembert* or *Brie* (the crust of which you can safely remove without causing offence) and countless goat cheeses *(fromage de chèvre),* some soft, some hard, some mild, some strong. Some restaurants will present you with a plate of pre-selected slices of cheese; at the other extreme, a waiter will show you a groaning cheese board. Don't hesitate to ask for names or simply to point at the cheese(s) of your choice. There are so many that even the French don't know their names and can't identify the varieties by sight. A *fromage blanc* – a tangy, fresh, low-fat cheese rather like yogurt – can be refreshing between a meat course and a sweet dessert.

For **desserts**, try a *mousse au chocolat* or *sorbet* (sherbet) – *cassis* (blackcurrant), *framboise* (raspberry) or *citron* (lemon). Or fruit tarts – *tarte aux abricots* (apricot), *aux fraises* (strawberry), or most magical of all, *tarte Tatin,* hot caramelised apples baked under a pastry crust – attributed to the Tatin sisters of Sologne after one of them accidentally dropped the tart upside down on the hotplate when taking it out of the oven.

Regional Cuisine

Once acquainted with these basics, you're ready to start your tour of the regional specialities. There's no specifically Parisian cuisine, but the capital is able to offer a sample of virtually everything you'll find around the country.

France boasts more than 365 cheeses

Picardy, for those coming in from the north, offers *flamique à porions,* a leek pie that is best served piping hot. Wonderful, filling vegetable soups are also typical of the region. In **Amiens**, make a point of trying the traditional *pâté de canard* (duck pâté).

Cuisine from **Alsace** is rich in freshwater fish and game, and offers a subtle mix of French, German, and even Jewish cooking. Wonders are performed with cabbage: *choucroute garnie* cooked in Riesling with juniper berries, a cup of Kirsch tossed in at the end, makes poetry out of sauerkraut and sausage. *Civet de lièvre* is a hare stew fit for a king, and *oie braisée aux pommes* (goose braised with apples) warms the cockles of the heart. The prince of Alsatian cheeses is Munster.

Tempting cakes

Burgundy, inspired by the high life led by its grand old dukes, is ideal for those with solid appetites. This wine-growing region produces the world's greatest beef stew, *bœuf bourguignon*: beef simmered in red wine for at least four hours with mushrooms, small white onions, and chunks of bacon. The tasty corn-fed poultry of Bresse is the aristocrat of French fowl and best enjoyed at its simplest, either roasted or steamed. Charolais beef, from the lovingly tended white cattle of southern Burgundy, produces the tenderest steaks. *A la dijonnaise* will usually mean a sauce of Dijon's mustard, distinctively flavoured by the sour juice of Burgundy grapes. *Jambon persillé* (ham with parsley) is another Dijon speciality. *Escargots* (snails) are now mostly imported from Eastern Europe in order to meet the heavy demand, but Burgundians still make the best butter, garlic, and parsley sauce for them – also used with *cuisses de grenouilles* (frogs' legs) from the Dombes region. Among the cheeses of Burgundy are the moist, orange-crusted *Epoisses* and *Soumaintrain*.

Normandy cuisine makes full use of the produce of the region's dairy farms. Indeed, cream and butter are staples of the cuisine – the secret behind the sumptuous *omelette de la mère Poulard* that you'll find at Mont-St-Michel. The rich and slightly sour *crème fraîche* also makes the perfect accompaniment to a hot apple pie. The local apples are also

Brittany oysters

featured in flambéed partridge *(perdreau flambé aux reinettes)* and in chicken with apple-brandy sauce *(poulet au Calvados).* Rouen, the capital of Normandy, is famous for its *caneton à la rouennaise,* a duckling of unusually deep-red meat with a spicy red-wine sauce thickened with minced duck livers. As well as *Camembert* cheese be sure to sample the stronger *Livarot* and square, tangy *Pont-l'Evêque.*

Brittany is best known for its magnificent seafood, often served fresh and unadorned on a bed of crushed ice and seaweed, a *plateau de fruits de mer.* This will include oysters *(huîtres),* various kinds of clams *(palourdes, praires),* mussels *(moules),* scallops *(coquilles Saint-Jacques),* succulent prawns *(langoustines),* winkles *(bigorneaux),* large whelks *(bulots)* and chewy abalones *(ormeaux).* Purists prefer their lobster *(homard)* simply steamed or grilled to retain its full, undisguised flavour. *Lobster à l'américaine* swims in a shellfish stock enriched with tomato, Cognac, cream and herbs.

The area is also known for the excellence of its pancakes – *crêpes* (usually sweet) and *galettes* (mostly savoury), both traditionally served with cider rather than wine.

In the **Loire Valley**, try the freshwater fish (eel, trout, pike or perch) cooked in a light *beurre blanc* (white butter sauce). A delicacy of the region is *matelote d'anguille* (eel stewed in red wine). *Rillettes* (a type of sausage) made from duck, goose or pork make another delectable appetiser. *Noisette de porc aux pruneaux* (tenderloin of pork with prunes) is a lusty main dish. One of the best goat cheeses in France is *Valençay*, shaped like an Aztec pyramid.

Lyon, the gastronomic capital of France, is renowned for the quality of its pork, wild game, vegetables and fruit. Onion soup *(soupe à l'oignon)* is a local invention, and *à la lyonnaise* most often means that a dish is sautéed in onions. If you have a robust stomach, you may fancy the *gras-double* (tripe) or *andouille,* a sausage made of chitterlings. More delicate dishes include, as appetisers, artichoke hearts *(cœurs d'artichaut)* with foie gras, or *gratin de queues d'écrevisses* (baked crayfish tails); as main dishes, leg of lamb braised for seven hours and *poularde demi-deuil* – chicken in 'semi-mourning', because of the white meat and black truffles.

The cuisine of **Bordeaux** exploits its wines. The *borde-laise* sauce is made with white or red wine, shallots and beef marrow, and is served variously with *entrecôte* steaks, *cèpe* mushrooms or lamprey eels *(lamproies)*. The oysters and mussels from nearby Arcachon are excellent. Try the region's Pauillac lamb *à la persillade* (cooked with parsley).

In **Languedoc-Roussillon** you will find *moules farcies* (stuffed mussels on a half-shell) and *bourride de bau-droie,* a stew of monkfish and

Escargots à l'ail, a French classic

A well-stocked cellar in St-Emilion

vegetables with garlic mayonnaise or *aïoli.*

Provence, embracing the Côte d'Azur, marries Mediterranean sea-food with garlic, olives, tomatoes and the country's most fragrant herbs. For an appetiser, have the local fresh sardines simply grilled and sprinkled with lemon. More spicy is *tapenade,* a mousse made of capers, anchovies, black olives, garlic and lemon.

From the coastal area between Marseille and Toulon comes *bouilla-baisse,* a fish stew that may contain some or all of the following: *rascasse* (scorpion fish), John Dory, eel, red mullet, whiting, perch, spiny lobster, crabs and other shellfish, seasoned with tomatoes, olive oil, garlic, bay leaf, parsley, pepper and, for true authenticity, saffron. Provençal cooks also make a splendid *daube de bœuf* (beef stew with tomatoes and olives).

Périgord is famous for its *pâté de foie gras,* truffles and its rich goose and duck dishes, most notably *confit d'oie* or *confit de canard.* The bird is cooked slowly in its own fat and kept for days, weeks or even months in earthenware jars. The *confit* is used as the base of the hearty Toulouse or Castelnaudary *cassoulet,* which includes beans, pork, mutton and sausage. And don't forget *pommes sarladaises,* potatoes sautéed in goose fat, garlic and parsley; dandelion salad *(salade de pissenlit)* dressed with walnut oil and bacon; and chestnuts, roasted and served with partridge or made into rich desserts.

WHAT TO DRINK

Apéritifs

Typical French choices for pre-dinner drinks would be a *pastis* (anise-flavoured liqueur), a *kir* (white wine, preferably a Burgundian aligoté, with a splash of blackcurrant liqueur), or a vermouth.

Wine, Beer and Water

The **Burgundy** reds divide into two categories, those that can be drunk relatively young – the supple *Côte de Beaune* wines of Aloxe-Corton, Pommard, and Volnay – and those that need to age a little, the full-bodied *Côte de Nuits* wines of Vougeot, Gevrey-Chambertin and Chambolle-Musigny. Outstanding Burgundy whites include Meursault and Puligny-Montrachet.

Bordeaux wines have four main regional divisions: Médoc, aromatic mellow red with a slight edge to it; Graves, an easy-to-drink red that's dry and vigorous like the Burgundies; Saint-Emilion, dark, strong, and full-bodied and the pale, golden Sauternes, sweet and fragrant and perfect with foie gras. The lesser Bordeaux wines can all be drunk a couple of years old, but good ones need at least five years to mature.

The **Loire Valley** produces dry white wines including Vouvray and Sancerre, and robust reds such as Bourgueil and Chinon.

Of the **Côtes du Rhône** wines, the best-known red is the fragrant, deep purple Châteauneuf-du-Pape, but look out for the Gigondas and Hermitage and, for lunchtime, the Tavel rosé.

The names of the delicious, often underestimated white wines of **Alsace** depend on the variety of grapes from which they are made – Gewürztraminer, Riesling or Sylvaner.

Note that if you prefer red rather than white wine, it is perfectly

Local apéritif, Gascony

acceptable to order red with fish; in fact a chilled Brouilly, Morgon or Chiroubles of the Beaujolais family would be an excellent accompaniment for both fish and meat. Dry Burgundy or Loire Valley whites are exquisite with fish. Beer goes particularly well with Toulouse sausage and Alsatian *choucroute*.

Tap water *(eau du robinet)* is safe to drink throughout France, and although the French do like a bottled mineral water with a meal sometimes, it's now accepted that, for the sake of the planet, ordering from the tap is fine. A common brand of still water *(eau minérale)* is Evian; a popular carbonated *(eau gazeuse)* type is Badoit.

Digestifs

For an after-dinner drink, as well as *Cognac* and the mellower *Armagnac*, there's a wide range of fruit brandies *(eaux-de-vie)* made from pear, plum, cherry or raspberry, as well as the famous apple *Calvados*. For a sparkling finish, splash out on the nation's pride and joy: Champagne, described by connoisseurs as *aimable, fin, et élégant* ('friendly, refined and elegant').

USEFUL PHRASES

Do you have a table? **Avez-vous une table?**
The bill, please **L'addition, s'il vous plaît**

TO HELP YOU ORDER...

I would like (a/an/the/some)… **J'aimerais…**

menu **la carte**
tea **du thé**
coffee **un café**
sugar **du sucre**
wine **du vin**
beer **une bière**
glass **un verre**

bread **du pain**
butter **du beurre**
milk **du lait**
salt **du sel**
pepper **du poivre**
meat **de la viande**
fish **du poisson**

...AND READ THE MENU

ail garlic
agneau lamb
asperges asparagus
bar sea bass
bœuf beef
caille quail
canard duck
cerises cherries
champignons mushrooms
chou cabbage
chou-fleur cauliflower
crevettes roses/grises
 prawns/shrimps
crudités raw vegetables
daurade sea bream
échalotes shallots
épinards spinach
farci stuffed
foie liver
fromage cheese
fruits de mer seafood
haricots verts green beans
homard lobster
huîtres oysters

jambon ham
langouste rock lobster
lapin rabbit
moules mussels
nouilles noodles
œufs eggs
oignons onions
petits pois peas
pintade guinea fowl
poché poached
poire pear
poireaux leeks
pomme apple
pomme de terre potato
porc pork
poulet chicken
raisins grapes
riz rice
rognon kidney
rôti roast
saucisse sausage
saumon salmon
thon tuna
veau veal

TRAVEL ESSENTIALS

PRACTICAL INFORMATION

A

ACCOMMODATION

Hotels. Hotels throughout France are officially classified from one-star to four-stars, and awarded according to the facilities and comfort offered but there is also the Palais distinction, designed to recognise the finest 5-star hotels in the country, and awarded by the ministry of tourism.

In many cases, hotels will ask for a deposit or credit card number before confirming a reservation. Breakfast is usually an optional extra. You can obtain lists of officially approved hotels throughout the country from the French national tourist office in your own country (see page 247). It usually benefits independent hoteliers to book directly through them rather than using an international online booking company.

When you arrive, tourist offices and syndicats d'initiative can supply local hotel lists and major airports and railway stations also have hotel reservation desks. You can also use Atout France (atout-france.fr), France's tourism development agency, to research accommodation. Note that a hotel labelled simply Hôtel may not have a restaurant.

Châteaux-Hôtels. These converted châteaux, spread across the whole of France, are an expensive but worthwhile romantic alternative, notably in the Loire Valley. Tourist offices will have directories.

Logis de France. These are government-approved hotels in the one- and two-star bracket; often outside towns, many with character and charm. Directories can be obtained from the French national tourist offices before leaving.

Pensions. These may be either small hotels or guest houses. They are generally family-owned and provide meals.

Gîtes de France and gîtes ruraux. These are officially sponsored, furnished self-catering accommodations ranging from holiday cottages or flats to on-farm campsites. Rental costs include all charges. Sleeping arrangements at gîtes that specialise in overnight stops and large groups may be in dormitories (couchage en bat flanc). Every département runs their own gîtes. The national organisation, Fédération Nationale des Gîtes de France, is at 40 avenue de Flandre, 75019 Paris (tel: 01 49 70 75 75; www.gites-de-france.com) and the website is very good.

House rental. Local tourist offices *(syndicats d'initiative)* can recommend agencies with complete lists of houses and apartments to let.

---

a double/single room **une chambre pour deux personnes/une personne**
with/without bath/shower **avec/sans baignoire/douche**
with a double bed/twin beds **avec un grand lit/deux lits**
What's the rate per night? **Quel est le prix pour une nuit ?**

AIRPORTS *(aéroports)*

Paris is the major gateway to France, but many international flights operate to other big cities and airports in other countries, such as Geneva, Basel, Brussels and Luxembourg, which may be better choices for some destinations in France. All French airports have duty-free shops and efficient transport to the town centre.

Paris is served by two airports: **Roissy-Charles-de-Gaulle (CDG)**, which is about 25km (15 miles) northeast of the city; and **Paris Orly (ORY)**, about 15km (9 miles) to the south. Most intercontinental flights use Roissy. For general information at Roissy airport, tel: 01 70 36 39 50. The official Paris airports website (www.adp.fr) gives detailed information, including diagrams of the various terminals and their services.

Buses take you from both airports into central Paris, and link the two airports. Buses from Roissy go to Porte de la Chapelle (journey time about 70 minutes/€6) and to Nation (80 minutes/€6). **Roissybus** offers services from Roissy to place de l'Opéra (60 minutes/€13.70). **Orlybus** goes from Orly to the place Denfert-Rochereau (20–30 minutes/€9.50).

Trains from Roissy to the Gare du Nord, Châtelet, Saint-Michel and Denfert-Rochereau (RER line B) leave every 15 minutes (35 minutes/€10.30). An automatic train called Orlyval leaves the airport every 5 to 7 minutes and connects with the Antony station of RER Line B, stopping at Denfert-Rochereau, Saint-Michel, Châtelet and Gare du Nord (complete journey €12.10). All trains run frequently from early morning to late at night. A TGV station at Roissy's Terminal 2 allows quick access to Lille, Lyon and the south.

Taxis from the airports to the centre of Paris are expensive (€30–70) for single passengers but worthwhile for three.

Where's the bus for…? **D'où part le bus pour…?**
Can you help me with my luggage? **Pouvez-vous m'aider à porter mes bagages ?**
How much is that? **Combien est-ce que ça coûte ?**

B

BICYCLE AND MOPED HIRE *(location de bicyclettes/mobylettes)*

Cycling is very popular in France, and there are more than 30,000km (18,600 miles) of marked cycling routes. For information, contact the Fédération Française de Cyclotourisme, tel: 01 49 35 69 00, www.ffc.fr. It's possible to rent bikes *(bicyclettes* or *vélos)* in Paris and other tourist spots. Try at the train station, the local tourist office, or look them up on the internet. You will need your passport or identity card, and you'll have to pay a deposit unless you hold a major credit card.

Under the city's 'Vélib' scheme, thousands of bikes and racks across Paris are available for instant hire. Simply buy a ticket online or swipe your Navigo Découverte pass and pedal away. Visit https://www.velib-metropole.fr/ for more details.

Bicycles can be carried free on some trains, including in the baggage cars of local trains in the Paris/Ile de France region outside rush hours. On TGV and some long-distance trains, bikes can be put in the luggage racks if they are folded or carried in bike bags with wheels removed. Call the SNCF on 36 35, www.sncf.com.

Mopeds (*mobylettes*) are sometimes available for rent as well (same conditions as for bikes). Minimum age to ride a moped is 14; for scooters from 50 to 125cc, it is 16; over 125cc, it's 18 (with some limits up to 21). Crash helmets are compulsory. Ask at your hotel or local tourist office

---

I'd like to rent a bicycle for one day/a week **Je voudrais louer une bicyclette pour une journée/une semaine**

BUDGETING FOR YOUR TRIP

Paris is an expensive city, even by European standards. Your accommodation and those pleasant beers on fashionable squares will cost you dear. Once out of the capital, things become more reasonable. To give you an idea of what to expect, below are some average prices in euros. However, inflation inevitably makes them approximate, and there are considerable regional and seasonal differences.

Flights to Paris: Flying with the low-cost airlines from the UK can be around €70 return, less at certain times.

Petrol: Unleaded petrol costs around €1.70 and diesel €1.80 per litre.

Three-course evening meal in a mid-range restaurant: €30–€50

Alcoholic and non-alcoholic drinks in bars/restaurants average price: (beer half litre €4.50–7; coffee €2.50–5, mineral water €2–4.

Hotel in Paris: (based on two sharing) luxury 4-star €300 and up, 4-star €170–300, 3-star €100–170, 2-star €70–100, 1-star €50–70.

Paris museum pass: 2-day 52, 4-day €66, 6-day €78.

Entry fees: museums: €5–15. Attractions such as aquarium in Boulogne cost €19.

C

CAMPING

For information about camping, pick up a leaflet from the tourist office. You can get your camping card, renewable annually, from the Fédération Française de Camping et de Caravaning, 78 Rue de Rivoli, 75004 Paris; tel: 01 42 72

84 08; www.ffcc.fr. Check for campsites on www.campingfrance.com or use an internet serach engine; lots of campsites have swanky websites these days.

Have you room for a tent/caravan? **Avez-vous de la place pour une tente/une caravane ?**

CAR HIRE *(location de voitures)*

Car hire in France is expensive (as much as €100 a day). Local companies may charge less than the international ones, but may be less flexible if you want to return the car elsewhere in the country. You can often find better deals online or if you book a car together with your plane or train ticket. It's cheaper if you reserve your car and pay in advance.

To rent a car you must produce a valid driving licence (held for at least one year) and your passport. Depending on the model and the rental company, the minimum age for renting a car varies from 21 to 26. Most agencies require payment by credit card. Third-party insurance is usually automatically included; for an additional charge per day you can obtain full insurance coverage.

I'd like to hire a car **Je voudrais louer une voiture**
tomorrow **demain**
for one day/a week **pour une journée/une semaine**
unlimited mileage **kilométrage illimité**
With full insurance **Avec assurance tous risques**

CLIMATE

Broadly, the further south you go the warmer it is. The northern and western areas of France (including Paris) enjoy a temperate climate. The region to the east and in the interior Massif Central has warmer summers and colder winters. The Mediterranean coastal area is characterised by hot, dry summers and mild, showery winters.

With the exception of this coast, rainfall is sporadic all year round, with the most precipitation between January and April and the least in August and September.

CRIME AND THEFT *(délit; vol)*

Use the same caution you would at home. Keep items of value in the hotel safe. Always lock your car and put valuables in the boot.

It's a good idea to be especially wary in the entertainment districts of large cities at night and to watch your wallet, handbag and backpack, especially in crowded airports, stations, buses and trains.

Any loss or theft should be reported as soon as possible to the nearest police station and to your embassy. Keep a copy of plane tickets and other personal documents, and a note of the phone number of your travel agent.

These days you should expect extra security checks at airports and entrances to the major attractions. Be aware that larger suitcases, travel bags and backpacks will not be permitted in many museums or left in cloakrooms.

> My ticket/wallet/passport has been stolen **On a volé mon billet/ portefeuille/passeport**

D

DRIVING

To take your car into France you will need:

Your national driving licence (minimum age 18)

Proof of ID (your passport will do)

Car registration papers

Insurance certificate (a green card is no longer obligatory, but comprehensive insurance coverage is advisable)

Crit'Air vignette – a clean air sticker that must be displayed when driving in some cities. From July 2023, only electric vehicles and vehicles of the Crit'Air 1 and Crit'Air 2 categories may drive in the Paris low emission zone Mon–Fri 8am-8pm.

All drivers must carry a high visibility jacket and a warning triangle *inside* their car, not in the boot.

All passengers must wear seat belts and motorcycle/scooter riders must wear helmets. Children under 10 must stay in the back seat.

Regulations. As elsewhere in Europe, drive on the right, overtake on the left and yield right-of-way to all vehicles coming from the right (except on round-abouts/traffic circles) unless otherwise indicated. Alcohol levels are strict (0.5 mg alcohol per 100ml of blood; the limit for drivers with less than three years of driving experience is 0.2 mg alcohol per 100ml of blood).

Speed limits. On dry roads: 130kph (80mph) on toll motorways, 110kph (68mph) on dual carriageways, 90kph (56mph) or 80kph (50mph) on all other roads, and 50kph (31mph) in built-up areas. When the roads are wet, the limit on motorways is reduced by 20kph, and on all other roads by 10kph (6mph).

Road conditions. French roads are designated by an A, standing for *auto-route* (motorway); an N for *nationale*, (national highway); a D for *départemen-tale* (regional road). Roads become very busy during peak holiday periods: around 1 and 14 July, 1 and 15 August, and 1 September. Rush hours in large towns usually last from 7.30 to 9am and from 5.30 to 7.30pm.

Tolls *(péage)* on the autoroutes are relatively expensive. Cash and major credit cards are accepted. For a more leisurely drive, take the alternative routes *(itinéraire bis)* signposted by arrows: a green arrow on a white background indicates north–south, while the opposite direction is shown by a white arrow on a green background.

Parking. In town centres, you will find that street parking places (usually marked *payant*) have their own individual meter or you will be required to display inside the car a ticket obtained from a machine *(horodateur)*, which will allow you to park for a specific period of time. Don't park where there are dotted yellow lines. Fines for parking violations are heavy; in serious cases your car may be towed away or have a wheel clamp attached. Many towns have introduced Zone Bleue parking zones, which allow you to park for a certain amount of time as long as you display your arrival time on a special blue parking disc, obtainable from tabacs and newsagents.

Breakdowns. Switch on flashing warning lights; place a warning triangle 30m (33yds) behind the car; put on your high-visibility jacket. There are emer-gency phones at regular intervals on main roads. The *gendarmerie* will send a breakdown service. It's wise to have internationally valid breakdown insurance, and to get an estimate before repairs are done. Value-added tax (TVA) will be additional to the estimate.

Accidents. Contact the police immediately. All parties should fill out and sign an accident form *(constat à l'amiable)* and exchange insurance details. If you rent a car, the form will be provided.

Petrol. The most common types of petrol *(essence)* are unleaded *(sans plomb)* or diesel *(gas-oil)*; leaded *(au plomb)* is sometimes available.

Priorité à droite Give way to traffic from right
Ralentir Slow down
Sauf riverains No entry except for residents
Sens interdit No entry
Sens unique One-way street
Serrez à droite/gauche Keep right/left
Sortie de camions Lorry exit
Stationnement interdit No parking
Véhicules lents Slow vehicles
Vous n'avez pas la priorité You do not have priority

E

ELECTRICITY

Electricity in France is 220 volt. You'll need an adapter for most plugs and US equipment will require a voltage transformer.

EMBASSIES AND CONSULATES *(ambassades; consulats)*

For major problems, such as loss of passport or all your money, serious accident or difficulties with the police, contact your embassy or consulate. All embassies are in Paris, with consulates in other cities. It's best to phone before visiting, as opening times vary.

Australia: 4 rue Jean-Rey, tel: 01 40 59 33 00, www.france.embassy. gov.au.

Canada: 139 rue du Faubourg Saint-Honoré tel: 01 44 43 29 00, https://www. international.gc.ca/country-pays/france/ .

Ireland: 12 avenue Foch, tel: 01 44 17 67 00, www.embassyofireland.fr.

New Zealand: 103 rue de Grenelle, tel: 01 45 01 43 43, https://www.mfat. govt.nz/

South Africa: 59 quai d'Orsay, tel: 01 53 59 23 23, www.afriquesud.net.

UK: 35 rue du Faubourg-St-Honoré, tel: 01 44 51 31 00, www.ukinfrance.fco. gov.uk.

US: 2 ave Gabriel, tel: 01 43 12 22 22, https://fr.usembassy.gov/

Where's the embassy/consulate? **Où se trouve l'ambassade/le consulat ?**

EMERGENCIES *(urgence)*

In emergencies, dial 15 for ambulance, 17 for the police *(police secours)*, or 18 for the fire brigade *(pompiers)*, 112 for European general emergencies.

Fire! **Au feu !**
Can you help me? **Pouvez-vous m'aider ?**

G

GAY AND LESBIAN TRAVELLERS

France is one of the most gay-friendly countries in Europe especially in the cities and in the laid-back south coast region. Paris Gay Pride is a world-famous parade and festival, which takes place every June. For information see www. gay-france.net and www.centrelgbtparis.org.

GETTING THERE (see also Airports)

By air. Paris is the major gateway to France and is served by two international airports, Roissy-Charles-de-Gaulle and Orly. Approximate journey times to Paris are: London 1 hour; New York 7 hours; Toronto 7 hours; and Johannesburg 11 hours. Budget airlines fly from airports all over Europe to over 20 airports in France with the internet the main method of booking. The main airlines currently offering flights include: www.easyjet.com, www.flybe.com, www.cityjet.com, as well as the long-haul fliers, such as: www.aa.com, www.airfrance.co.uk and www.britishairways.com.

Most tour operators charter seats on scheduled flights at a reduced price as part of a package deal. Wine tasting, gourmet and cooking tours, as well as tours of the châteaux, are usually included in package deals.

By car. Cross-channel choices include ferries, high-speed catamarans and the Channel Tunnel – with a wide variety of prices, schedules and arrival ports. Travel via the tunnel is fastest (35 minutes) and offers frequent departures each way between Folkestone and Calais, 24 hours a day.

By bus. Regular services operate from London to Paris (via Calais). Numerous lines join Paris with cities such as Bordeaux, Lyon or Nice.

By rail. All the main lines converge on Paris. There's an excellent network of express and high-speed TGV (*train à grande vitesse*) trains. First-class and second-class fares are available (a supplement is payable on certain trains); advance booking is compulsory. Trains from Paris to Lille take 1 hour; Paris–Lyon 2 hours; Paris–Besançon 2.5 hours; Paris–Avignon 2½ hours; and Lille–Lyon 4 hours. The journey from London to Paris takes from 6 to 11 hours with a ferry crossing, only 3 hours via the Channel Tunnel.

Tickets from the UK: An InterRail France pass offers a month's unlimited rail travel in France on a certain number of days (three, four, six or eight), either consecutively or spread out. Concessions for children and the elderly are available.

Tickets from the US: An InterRail France pass offers continuous, unlimited rail travel for 2, 4, 5, 8 or 15 days; a flexi pass offers the choice of 1, 2, 3, 4, 5, 6, 7, 8, or 9 days within a one-month period. Discounts for travellers under 26 and over 60 are available. Many of these must be purchased before you leave home. You can find information at www.raileurope.com.

H

HEALTH AND MEDICAL CARE

Make sure your health insurance covers illness or accident abroad. Your insurance representative, automobile association or travel agent can give you details of special travel insurance.

Visitors from European Union countries with corresponding health insurance facilities are entitled to medical and hospital treatment under the French social security system. You must have your European Health Insurance Card (EHIC) card with you for reciprocal health care. Post-Brexit, visitors from the UK can use their EHIC cards until they expire, at which point they should apply for the new GHIC card.

If you need a doctor or dentist, ask for advice at your hotel, the *syndicat d'initiative* or the local police station *(gendarmerie)*.

Doctors who belong to the French social security system *(médecins conventionnés)* charge the minimum rate. It is fine to ask what the fee will be before making an appointment.

French doctors may not always speak English. They will, however, understand some English medical terms.

Where's the nearest (all-night) chemist? **Où se trouve la pharmacie (de garde) la plus proche ?**
I need a doctor/dentist **Il me faut un médecin/dentiste**
I feel sick **J'ai mal au cœur**
I have a headache **J'ai mal à la tête**
stomach ache **mal à l'estomac**
fever **de la fièvre**

Chemists *(pharmacies)*. These are easily recognised by a green cross hanging outside. The staff are helpful in dealing with minor ailments but often don't speak English. This can be difficult as most medications are not on display and you will have to ask for them or describe your symptoms. It's helpful to look up a few words in a dictionary before going. There's always a chemist on night-duty; the address will be displayed in the window of other pharmacies.

L

LANGUAGE

You'll find the French are much more welcoming to tourists who make an effort to speak French, even if it's only the odd word badly pronounced - it is definitely the thought that counts. Rough Guides has a free-to-download phrasebook app that is pre-loaded with 12 languages including French. It includes a travel dictionary, menu reader, need-to-know phrases and more useful functions. Visit www.books.roughguides.com/phrasebook-downloads for more.

good morning/good afternoon **bonjour**
good afternoon/good evening **bonsoir**
good bye **au revoir**
Is there anyone here who speaks English? **Y a-t-il quelqu'un ici
    qui parle anglais ?**
yes/no **oui/non**
please/thank you **s'il vous plaît/merci**
excuse me **excusez-moi**
where?/when?/how? **où ?/quand?/comment ?**
how much? **combien ?**
old/new **vieux/neuf**
yesterday/today/tomorrow **hier/aujourd'hui/demain**
left/right **gauche/droite**
up/down **en haut/en bas**
good/bad **bon/mauvais**

big/small **grand/petit**
cheap/expensive **bon marché/cher**
hot/cold **chaud/froid**
old/new **vieux/neuf**

M

MAPS

Small street maps *(plans)* are given away at tourist offices and by many hotels. You can buy detailed country or regional maps *(cartes)* in bookshops and at news-stands.

MEDIA

In addition to French national and local newspapers *(journaux)*, you'll find the Paris-based *International Herald Tribune, Wall Street Journal,* and many British daily papers in major cities all over France, usually on publication day. Magazines in many languages are available at larger news-stands.

There are several national and cable TV channels.

MONEY

Currency. France's unit of currency is the *euro* (€), which is divided into 100 cents. Coins *(pièces)* come in 1, 2, 5, 10, 20 and 50 cents; 1 and 2 euros. Banknotes *(billets)* come in 5, 10, 20, 50, 100, 200 and 500 euros.

Could you give me some change? **Pouvez-vous me donner de la monnaie ?**
I want to change some pounds/dollars **Je voudrais changer des livres sterling/des dollars**
Do you accept travellers' cheques? **Acceptez-vous les chèques de voyage ?**

Banks and bureaux de change. Hours may vary, but most Paris banks are open from 9am to 5pm Monday to Friday; in smaller places they may close for an hour or two at lunchtime and may open on Saturdays for several hours and close on Mondays. Some bureaux de change operate on Saturdays. Your hotel will usually change currency, but the rate will not be the most unfavourable. Always take your passport along when you go to change money. Note that small towns don't always have a bank.

OPENING TIMES

Office workers tend to start work at around 8am or 9am and work the stand-ard 35-hour week, finishing at around 5 or 6pm but accruing additional an-nual leave as a result of the extra time worked each day.

Lunch is served from noon or 12.30pm until 2pm, after which, it will be difficult to get anything outside of what is on offer at a supermarket or boulangerie.

Outside the major towns, even supermarkets and petrol stations shut for a few hours, so plan your shopping to avoid getting caught without fuel or food. Dinner is usually available from 6pm or later, and 8pm is a popular time.

Sunday **dimanche**
Monday **lundi**
Tuesday **mardi**
Wednesday **mercredi**
Thursday **jeudi**
Friday **vendredi**
Saturday **samedi**
open **ouvert**
closed **fermé**

P

POLICE

Most tourists find the French police friendly, intelligent and helpful. Dial 17 anywhere in France for police help. In cities and large towns you'll see the blue-uniformed *police municipale*, the local police force who keep order, investigate crime and direct traffic. In the country, *gendarmes* are responsible for traffic control and crime investigation.

> Where's the nearest police station? **Où est le poste de police le plus proche ?**

POST OFFICES *(bureau de poste)*

You can identify French post offices by a sign with a stylised blue bird on a yellow background and/or the words *La Poste*. In cities, the main post office is open from 8am to 7pm on weekdays and 8am to noon on Saturdays. In smaller towns, weekday hours may be 9am to noon and 2 to 6pm. In Paris, the Poste du Louvre, 50 rue du Louvre, is open 8am–midnight, 7 days a week. Major post offices can cash or send international postal and money orders, and have fax and telephone facilities.

Letterboxes in France are painted yellow and often set into a wall. Stamps *(timbres)* can be bought at post offices, as well as at *tabacs* (tobacconists).

> express (special delivery) **exprès**
> airmail **par avion**
> registered **recommandé**
> A stamp for this letter/ postcard, please **Un timbre pour cette lettre/carte, s'il vous plaît**

Poste restante. If you don't know where you'll be staying, you can have your mail addressed to you *c/o poste restante* in any town. Towns with more than one post office keep mail at the main office *(poste principale)*. You'll have to show your passport and pay a small charge to retrieve your mail.

PUBLIC HOLIDAYS

French national holidays cause large traffic jams on the eve. When one falls on a Tuesday or Thursday, the French often take Monday or Friday off to make a long weekend, known as a *pont* (bridge).

1 January *Jour de l'an* New Year's Day
1 May *Fête du Travail* Labour Day
8 May *Armistice 1945* VE Day
14 July *Fête nationale* Bastille Day
15 August *Assomption* Assumption
1 November *Toussaint* All Saints' Day
11 November *Armistice 1918* Armistice Day
25 December *Noël* Christmas Day
Movable dates: *Lundi de Pâques* Easter Monday
Ascension Ascension
Lundi de Pentecôte Whit Monday

T

TELEPHONES *(téléphones)*

Long-distance and international calls can be made from any phone box. If you make a call from your hotel, a café or a restaurant, charges may be higher than from a public telephone.

Most pay phones, which are now scarce, are card-operated. You can buy phone cards *(télécartes)* at post offices, souvenir shops and *tabacs*; they are available for 50 or 120 units. Most pay phones accept credit cards and the call is charged to your account. For long-distance calls within France, there are no area codes (you just dial the 10-digit number). For information, dial 12.

For international calls from France, dial 00 followed, after the change of tone, by the country code (listed in all public phone boxes), the area code and number. For an international operator dial 00, then 33, followed by the country's number (UK 44, US and Canada 1). For international inquiries, dial 00 33 12, followed by the country code number.

The cost of using your mobile phone depends on the roaming rates of your provider so check before you leave.

TIME DIFFERENCES

France follows Central European Time (Greenwich Mean Time +1). In the spring clocks are put forward 1 hour, and back 1 hour in autumn.

TIPPING

A 10 percent service charge is included automatically in restaurant bills *(service compris)*. Rounding off the overall bill by a euro or two helps round off friendships with waiters, too. It is considered normal to hand porters, doormen and petrol station attendants a coin or two for their services.

Porter and hotel room staff, per bag/day €2

Waiter 2–3 percent

Taxi driver 10–15 percent

Tour guide/bus driver €2–3

TOILETS *(toilettes)*

Public conveniences in France range from the 'footpad and hole-in-the-ground' variety to luxury three-star facilities. It's advisable to use toilets in cafés rather than any public facilities, though facilities operated by municipalities can be very clean. A saucer with small change on it means that a tip is expected. *Sanisettes* are high-tech outdoor cubicles that clean and disinfect themselves after use.

Women's toilets will be marked *Dames* or *Femmes;* men's will be marked either *Messieurs* or *Hommes*.

> Where are the toilets please? **Où sont les toilettes, s'il vous plaît?**

TOURIST INFORMATION

The French Tourism Development Agency is called Atout France (www.france.fr/fr) and its website has useful advice on accommodation, places to visit and transport, as well as links to tourist organisations and companies.

Australia and New Zealand: Level 13, 25 Bligh Street, Sydney, NSW 2000, tel: 2 9210-5400; http://au.france.fr.

Canada: 1800 avenue McGill Collège, Bureau 1010, Montreal, Québec H3A 3J6; tel: 1 514 288 20 26; http://ca.france.fr.

South Africa: Block C, Morningside Close, 222 Rivonia Road, Morningside, Johannesburg 2196, tel: 27 10 205 02 01.

UK: Lincoln House, 300 High Holborn, London WC1V 7JH, tel: 44 207 061 66 00, http://uk.france.fr.

US: There is just one Atout France office in the United States, no callers but write to 825 Third Avenue, 29th Floor, New York, NY 10022, http://us.france.fr.

Each sizeable town or tourist destination has its own *syndicat d'initiative*. They are invaluable sources of information, from maps to local hotel lists. The staff (often English-speaking) are extremely helpful. They don't generally recommend restaurants or make hotel reservations.

Syndicats d'initiative are usually found near to the centre of town, and often there is also a branch at the railway station. Opening hours vary, but the general rule is 9am to noon and 2 to 6 pm, every day except Sunday.

The main tourist office in Paris is in the north wing of the Hôtel de Ville, entrance at 29 rue de Rivoli, metro stop Hôtel de Ville. It's open daily from 9am-7pm apart from Christmas Day.

TRANSPORT

Tourist tickets. Many cities have special tourist tickets. In Paris, the *Paris Visite* pass allows unlimited travel on bus, métro, the Montmartre funicular and suburban (RER) trains for one, two, three or five consecutive days. Other options are available.

Buses (*autobus, autocar*). Large towns and cities have urban bus services – a particularly good way to get around and sightsee as you go. Inter-city bus services are efficient, comfortable, inexpensive and fairly frequent; the terminals are often situated close to the railway station, where you'll find timetables and other information.

Taxis. In large towns, there are taxi stands at the stations as well as in the centre, or you can hail a cab in the street. They're available only when the *Taxi* sign is fully lit up. Taxis can be called by telephone everywhere – local tourist offices will be able to give phone numbers or you can search on the internet. Rates vary from place to place and according to the time of day.

Métro. The Paris underground is one of the world's most efficient and fastest. It runs Sun–Thu from 5.30am to 1.15am and until 2am Fri–Sat, and at peak hours the trains run every minute. Buy books of 10 or 20 tickets *(carnet)* or, if you plan to take the *métro* or other means of public transport several times, a one, two, three or five-day travel pass, or a one-week or one-month Navigo Découverte Pass. Visit www.ratp.fr for information on travel in the Paris and the Ile de France area. Punch your ticket before boarding and keep it handy; you may have to show it to an inspector and you sometimes need them to exit turnstiles. There is also a metro in Lille, Lyon, Marseille, Toulouse, Strasbourg and Rouen.

Paris suburban trains *(Réseau Express Régional)*. The system of suburban lines (RER) is divided into five main lines (A, B, C, D, E) and provides express service between Paris and the suburbs. You can get across Paris in about 15 minutes, with a few stops in between. You can transfer to the RER at train and some *métro* stations.

Trains. SNCF *(Société Nationale des Chemins de Fer)* The French national railways run fast, clean and efficient trains. They have excellent regular services, often backed up by a network of SNCF-operated bus and coach services. Visit www.sncf.fr for further information.

---

one-way (single) **aller-simple**
round-trip (return) **aller-retour**
first/second class **première/seconde classe**
I'd like to reserve some seats **Je voudrais réserver des places**

Trams. Grenoble, Bordeaux, St-Etienne, Strasbourg, Nice, Nantes, Brest, Toulouse and Reims are among many French cities with modern tram networks that criss-cross the city. Tickets are available on board, in tobacco shops and at stops (automatic ticket distributors).

Aeroplanes. Air France, easyJet and other short-haul carriers fly between Paris and 29 regional airports, and link provincial cities.

V

VISAS AND ENTRY REQUIREMENTS

Nationals of European Union countries and Switzerland need only a valid passport or identity document to enter France. Nationals from the UK, Canada, New Zealand and the US require passports, and Australian and South African nationals must obtain a visa. For the latest information on entry requirements, contact the French Embassy in your country.

It's a good idea to have copies of prescriptions handy in case Customs (*douane*) asks you to account for any controlled substances.

Currency restrictions. For residents of non-EU countries, there's no limit on the import or export of local or foreign currencies or travellers' cheques, but amounts exceeding €10,000 must be declared.

In theory there are no customs limits within the EU for alcohol or tobacco, providing it is for personal requirements (generally calculated as a maximum of 10 litres of spirits, 20 litres of fortified wine, 90 litres of wine, 110 litres of beer, 200 cigars or 800 cigarettes) From outside the EU, the limits are 200 cigarettes, 1 litre of spirits and 2 litres of wine.

I've nothing to declare **Je n'ai rien à déclarer**
It's for my own use **C'est pour mon usage personnel**

W

WEBSITES

A selection of useful websites:

Disabled Travellers: https://uk.france.fr/en/holiday-prep/travelling-around-france-disability; ncf.com/en/passenger-offer/travel-for-everyone/accessibility; https://en.parisinfo.com/what-to-see-in-paris/visiting-paris-with-a-disability

French-English dictionary: www.freedict.com/onldict/fre.html

Museums and monuments: www.monuments-nationaux.fr/en

Road maps: www.google.com/maps

Tourist board: http://uk.france.fr

Train routes and times: www.sncf.com

Tours: www.francealacarte.com

Weather: http://france.meteofrance.com

INDEX

THE **MINI** ROUGH GUIDE TO **FRANCE**

First Edition 2023

Editor: Kate Drynan
Author: Rachel Ifans
Picture Editor: Tom Smyth
Cartography Update: Carte
Layout: Greg Madejak
Head of DTP and Pre-Press: Rebeka Davies
Head of Publishing: Sarah Clark
Photography Credits: Bigstock 90; Bill Wassman 18; Corbis 36; Dreamstime 22, 28, 83, 107, 109, 110, 120, 121, 124, 135, 141, 158, 164, 171, 172, 174, 181, 189, 211, 225; Emmanuel Berthier/Comité régional du tourisme de Bretagne 7B; Fotolia 21, 81, 149, 201; Getty Images 33; Ilpo Musto/Apa Publications 68; iStock 4TL, 5T, 5M, 6T, 17, 52, 111, 143; Kevin Cummins/Apa Publications 25, 62, 75, 76, 78, 79, 218, 219; Ming Tang-Evans/Apa Publications 31, 37, 44, 48, 50, 51, 53, 54, 56, 59, 60, 65, 70, 73, 74; Public domain 4ML, 27; Shutterstock 1, 4ML, 5T,5M, 5M, 5M, 5T, 6B, 7T, 11, 12, 14, 38, 47, 67, 82, 150, 156; Sylvaine Poitau/Apa Publications 34, 84, 86, 89, 93, 94, 97, 98, 101, 102, 105, 106, 112, 115, 116, 118, 123, 125, 127, 129, 131, 133, 136, 138, 139, 144, 147, 152, 155, 161, 163, 169, 170, 176, 177, 179, 183, 185, 187, 191, 192, 194, 195, 196, 198, 202, 204, 206, 208, 212, 214, 216, 220, 222, 223, 224, 226, 228; Wadey James/Apa Publications 40, 166
Cover Credits: Saint-Cirq-Lapopie **Jon Chica/Shutterstock**

Distribution
UK, Ireland and Europe: Apa Publications (UK) Ltd; sales@roughguides.com
United States and Canada: Ingram Publisher Services; ips@ingramcontent.com

Australia and New Zealand: Booktopia; retailer@booktopia.com.au
Worldwide: Apa Publications (UK) Ltd; sales@roughguides.com

Special Sales, Content Licensing and CoPublishing
Rough Guides can be purchased in bulk quantities at discounted prices. We can create special editions, personalised jackets and corporate imprints tailored to your needs. sales@roughguides.com; http://roughguides.com

Contact us
Every effort has been made to provide accurate information in this publication, but changes are inevitable. The publisher cannot be held responsible for any resulting loss, inconvenience or injury sustained by any traveller as a result of information or advice contained in the guide. We would appreciate it if readers would call our attention to any errors or outdated information, or if you feel we've left something out. Please send your comments with the subject line "Rough Guide Mini France Update" to mail@uk.roughguides.com.